Microsoft®
Visual C#®
2005 Express Edition
Programming
for the Absolute
Beginner

Microsoft® Visual C#®

2005 Express Edition Programming for the Absolute Beginner

ANEESHA BAKHARIA

THOMSON

COURSE TECHNOLOGY

Professional ■ Technical ■ Reference

ISBN: 1-59200-818-6
Library of Congress Catalog Card Number: 2005923963
Printed in the United States of America
06 07 08 09 10 PH 10 9 8 7 6 5 4 3 2

THOMSON

COURSE TECHNOLOGY
Professional ■ Technical ■ Reference

Thomson Course Technology PTR,
a division of Thomson Course Technology
25 Thomson Place
Boston, MA 02210
http://www.courseptr.com

Publisher and General Manager, Thomson Course Technology PTR: Stacy L. Hiquet

Associate Director of Marketing: Sarah O'Donnell

Manager of Editorial Services: Heather Talbot

Marketing Manager: Heather Hurley

Acquisitions Editor: Mitzi Koontz

Marketing Coordinator: Jordan Casey

Project Editor: Daniele Paulding Argosy Publishing

Technical Reviewer: Brian Lich

Thomson Course Technology PTR Editorial Services Coordinator: Elizabeth Furbish

Copyeditor: Bill McManus

Interior Layout Tech: Marian Hartsough

Cover Designer: Mike Tanamachi

Indexer: Sharon Shock

Proofreader: Marta Justak

This book is dedicated to my Grandmother,
who looked after me before I started school,
took me on many great holidays,
and raised 8 children.

Acknowledgments

I would like to thank:

- My Grandmother (Rada), my Dad (Abdulah) and my Mum (Juleka), my aunts (Kulsum, Julie, Hajira and Shaida), my uncles (Ebrahem, Rashid and Cassim) and my cousins (Celine, Zaeem and Tess) for their continued support and encouragement.

- Mitzi Koontz (Acquisitions Editor) for her continued support, dedication and enthusiasm.

- Daniele Paulding (Project Editor) for her patience, direction and flexibility.

- Bill McManus (Copyeditor) and Brian Lich (Technical Editor) for their excellent feedback and suggestions.

- Marian Hartsough (Layout), Marta Justak (Proofreading), Heather Talbot, and Kevin Sullivan.

- Madonna for making great music to listen to while writing.

ABOUT THE AUTHOR

ANEESHA BAKHARIA is a Web developer and accomplished author. She is fluent in C#, Java, JavaScript, ASP.NET, JSP, HTML, XML, and VB.NET. Aneesha specializes in creating dynamic database-driven Web sites. She has a Bachelor of Engineering degree in Microelectronic Engineering and various postgraduate qualifications in multimedia, online course development, and Web design. In addition to *Microsoft C# Fast & Easy Web Development*, she has written several other books for Course Technology PTR, including: *Dreamweaver MX 2004 Fast & Easy Web Development* (ISBN: 0761531645), *JavaServer Pages Fast & Easy Web Development* (ISBN: 0761534288) and *Pinnacle Studio 9 Ignite!* (ISBN: 159200475X). Aneesha lives in Brisbane, Australia, and is a big Madonna fan.

CONTENTS

Chapter 6 **DRAWING GRAPHICS AND BUILDING GAMES 119**

Chapter 7 **DESIGNING ADVANCED WINDOWS FORMS APPLICATIONS 139**

Chapter 8   OBJECT-ORIENTED PROGRAMMING FOR THE ABSOLUTE BEGINNER .161

Chapter 9   WORKING WITH DATABASES .173

INTRODUCTION

WELCOME TO VISUAL C# 2005 EXPRESS EDITION FOR THE ABSOLUTE BEGINNER

Thank you for purchasing this book. It is with great fondness that I remember the first programming book that I read. The book set me on a journey that would eventually lead me down the path of writing programming books myself. Learning to program is both challenging and rewarding. I hope this book inspires you to create great software.

Chapter 1: Getting Started with Visual C# Express

This chapter illustrates what a beginner can accomplish with Visual C# 2005 Express Edition. We'll be building an image viewer as well as a spiced up version the traditional "Hello World" beginner's application.

Chapter 2: C# Basics

In Chapter 2, we take a look at basic C# syntax and concepts. C# is the ideal beginner's language. C# has a simple syntax but is also very powerful. The Math Game, a game to test your ability to perform simple arithmetic operations will be covered in Chapter 2.

Chapter 3: Controlling Code Flow

If statements and for loops are covered. Don't worry if you don't know what if statements and for loops are because it will all become clear after reading this chapter. Essentially, if statements facilitate branching and decision making whereas for loops repeat the execution of code. A quiz will be designed and built in this chapter.

Chapter 4: Designing a User Interface

In this chapter you'll be impressed at how easy it is to construct a user interface. Visual C# 2005 Express Edition includes a plethora of interface controls. We'll concentrate on common interface elements such as Buttons, Labels and TextBoxes.

Chapter 5: Strings, Random Numbers, and Arrays

In Chapter 5, we have a challenging project. We will be designing and building a Word Finder puzzle generator. The key concepts to generate the puzzle, such as arrays and random numbers, will be covered. We'll also learn more about C# syntax and variables.

Chapter 6: Drawing Graphics and Building Games

This is a fun chapter. The chapter begins with an overview of graphics handling in C# and drawing various shapes onto a form. We then move on to simple animation and mouse control. Collision detection is presented in a very simple manner. We will use the concepts introduced in this chapter to design and build a single-player Pong game.

Chapter 7: Designing Advanced Windows Forms Applications

We take a look at some of the more advanced interface elements that are available in Visual C# Express Edition. Trees, tabs, menus and toolbars are all covered. We also explore the use of a Timer control to create a simple digital clock. You'll be able to build an application that allows users to draw simple shapes.

Chapter 8: Object-Oriented Programming for the Absolute Beginner

C# is an object-oriented language. In Chapter 8 we investigate object-oriented programming and work with a few simple code examples. Key concepts such as encapsulation and inheritance are covered.

Chapter 9: Working with Databases

This chapter provides a basic introduction to relational databases and using Visual C# Express Edition to database applications. Databases provide an easy way to store, update and query structured data. The Structured Query Language (SQL) will be used to query Microsoft Access databases. We will be building C# applications to display search results, as well as edit, insert and delete records in a database.

Chapter 10: Error Handling and Debugging

We won't be building an application in this chapter. Chapter 10 focuses on developing your debugging skills. You will be given a Tic-Tac-Toe game that has logical errors and will be asked to review and debug the code. You will also learn to use a debugger and write exception handling code.

Chapter 11: Reading and Writing Files

We'll be building a simple text editor in this chapter. The core .NET classes for saving and manipulating files and folders are also introduced. The file open and close dialog boxes will be used within the simple text editor project. To complete this chapter we will build a rich text editor that can save and open .rtf files.

Note

The source code for each project in this book can be downloaded from the Course Technology Web site: http://www.courseptr.com.

GETTING STARTED WITH VISUAL C# EXPRESS

As you read this paragraph, you are starting an amazing adventure. Learning to program changes your life. You will no longer just use software—you'll be inspired to create exciting games and feature-rich applications of your own. Visual C# 2005 Express Edition ("Visual C# Express" for short) is the ideal beginner's companion. Visual C# Express has tools to help you design an interface for your application and even show you where you need to add C# code. With Visual C# Express, programming is much easier than you think. By the end of this chapter, you'll have created a few very impressive applications. In this chapter, you will learn how to:

- Install Visual C# Express.
- Create, open, and save Visual C# Express projects.
- Design a graphical user interface.
- Build a simple "Hello World" Windows Forms application.
- Build a simple "Hello World" console-based application.
- Build an application that displays pictures.

PROJECT PREVIEW: THE PICTURE VIEWER

There is no better way to learn than to learn by doing. In each chapter, you'll learn key programming concepts and then utilize those key skills to build a fully functional game or application. This chapter is no exception, even though it is the first chapter in this book and you probably don't know how to program in C#. Don't worry, because you'll finish this chapter with a bang by building a Windows application that will impress family and friends.

The Picture Viewer application (see Figure 1-1) is a Windows Forms application that displays an image. The image is displayed on a Windows form. The main application window, which is really just a single form, works like any normal Microsoft Windows application that has a title bar, including Maximize and Close buttons in the upper-right corner.

The application will display a default image, but the user will also be able to use an Open dialog box to select another image (see Figure 1-2). The application is capable of displaying a variety of well-known image formats, including GIFs, JPEGs, and BMPs. The Picture Viewer application will also include a button to exit the application.

FIGURE 1-1

The Picture
Viewer
application.

FIGURE 1-2

The File Open
dialog box is used
to select an
image.

INSTALLING VISUAL C# EXPRESS

It's time to get your copy of Visual C# Express. It is possible to program C# programs in Notepad, but Visual C# Express helps you to write C# code, design intuitive visual interfaces, and debug and distribute your applications. Visual C# Express also improves your productivity once you're a well-accomplished C# programmer.

You obtain Visual C# Express from the Visual Studio 2005 Express Products Web page (**http://msdn.microsoft.com/vstudio/express/**), which contains links to each product in the Express product range, including Visual C# 2005 Express Edition, Visual Basic 2005 Express Edition, and Visual J# 2005 Express Edition. You need to click on the Visual C# 2005 Express link to open the download page for Visual C# Express, shown in Figure 1-3. Click on the Download Now button, and you will be prompted to download the VCSSetup.exe file, which is only 2.34MB in size. After the file has been downloaded and executed, a wizard will guide you through the installation process and download a further 400MB of applications and components. You'll also be prompted to install additional help (MSDN Express Library) and SQL Server Express, a free database server. The .NET Framework version 2.0 is also installed.

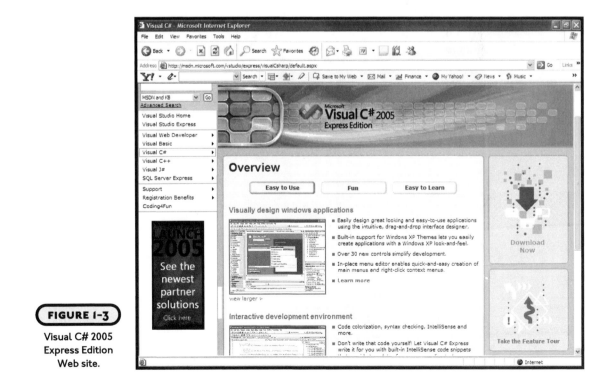

FIGURE 1-3

Visual C# 2005 Express Edition Web site.

CREATING A VISUAL HELLO WORLD APPLICATION

Now the fun begins—you get to create your first C# program. Your first application is a modern version of the traditional "Hello World" application, which simply writes a line of text to the command line. The Visual Hello World application will display "Hello World" in a large, attractive font. You will also improve the visual appeal of the form by displaying an image. The final functionality your first application will include is the ability to ask users for their name and then, based on their response, personalize the "Hello World" text.

1. Click Start, All Programs, Visual C# 2005 Express Edition. The Visual C# 2005 Express Edition application will open.

2. Click File, New Project. The New Project dialog box opens, shown in Figure 1-4. As you can see, there are several different types of C# applications that you can create from the installed templates, including a Windows application, a console application, and a screen saver. The Visual Hello World application that we are creating is going to have a graphical interface (as its name implies), so we need to create a Windows application.

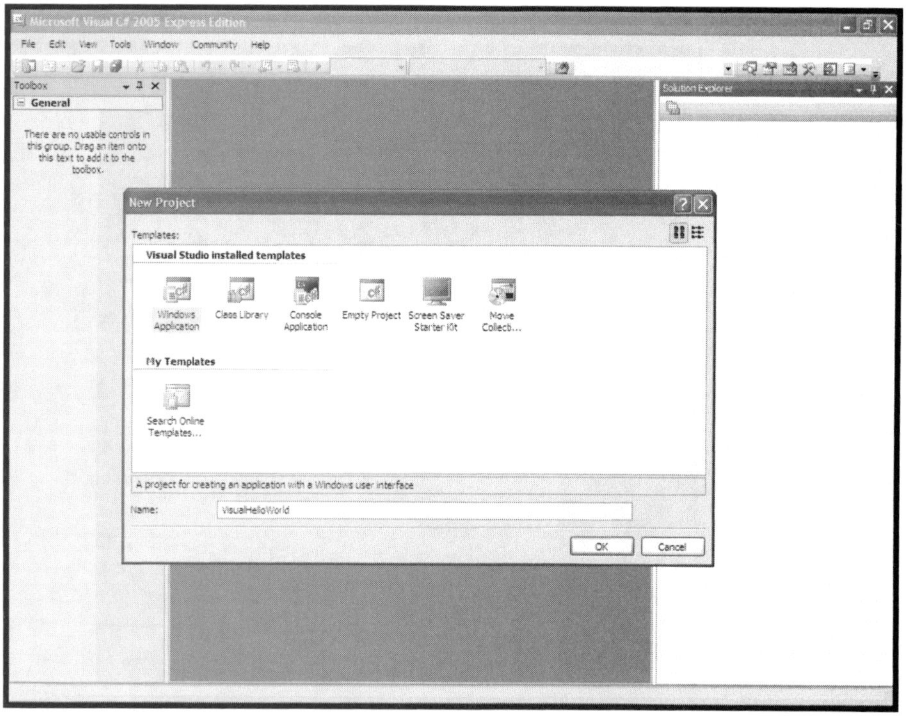

FIGURE 1-4

The New Project dialog box.

3. Select Windows Application as the project type.

4. Enter **VisualHelloWorld** as the application name in the Name field.

5. Click OK. A new Windows application project will be created in a new folder. A blank form will also be displayed in the Windows Form window (see Figure 1-5). We'll design the interface for our application by adding buttons, text, and images to this form. The size of the form is quite small, so we need to make it bigger.

6. Click on the bottom-right corner of the blank form. The cursor will change to a double-headed arrow. Drag the corner of the form to make it larger.

7. The title of the form simply says Form1, but you can change it. In fact, the title is one of numerous properties that you can configure for a form. You can view and edit each property in the Properties window (see Figure 1-6). Click on the form to make it active; then click View, Properties Window. The Properties window opens and displays all the properties associated with a form. The Text property contains the text that is displayed in the title bar.

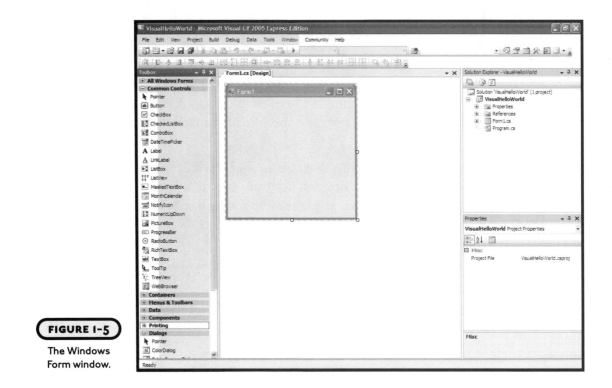

FIGURE 1-5

The Windows Form window.

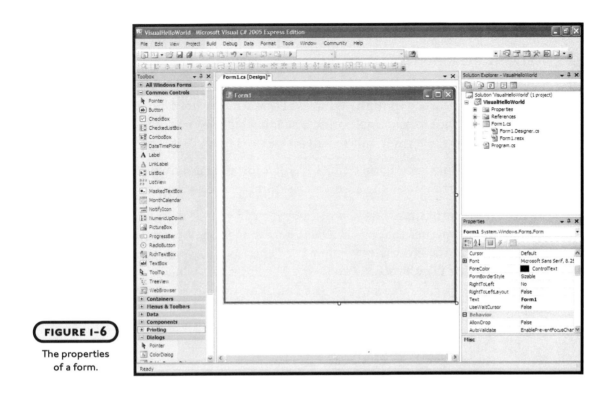

FIGURE 1-6

The properties
of a form.

8. Change the Windows Form title from Form1 by selecting the Text property, as shown in Figure 1-6, and changing the value in the column next to it to **Hello World**. Press Enter after you have changed the text, and the title of the form will reflect the changes that you have made.

9. The Toolbox displays all the controls that can be added to a form. Controls are grouped into categories, such as Common Controls, Menus & Toolbars, and Dialogs. You'll find everything from buttons to menus and dialog boxes. Scroll through the list of Common Controls. There is even a Web browser control.

10. Drag a Label control from the Toolbox to the top of the form.

11. Change the Text property of the label from label1 to **Hello World**.

12. Change the Font property by clicking on the Build button. A dialog box changes the font and font size of the text (see Figure 1-7).

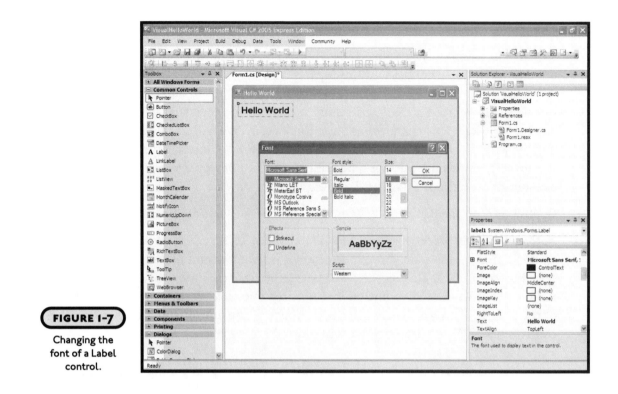

FIGURE 1-7

Changing the font of a Label control.

13. Drag a PictureBox control onto the form. The PictureBox control, as its name suggests, displays an image on a form.

14. Click on the right column of the Image property. A button with three periods is displayed. Click on this button to display the Select Resource window. Click on the Import button to navigate to and select an image from your hard drive. The image will be added as an Entry in the Select Resource window. Click on OK to assign the image, referenced by its path to the Image property of the PictureBox control.

15. Resize the PictureBox control if its size is either too large or too small to display the image you want to display.

    The application is certainly starting to take shape. The next thing we are going to do is add a Say Hello button and add some code that will ask users to enter their name and then, based on their input, personalize the Hello World text.

16. Drag a Button control onto the form.

17. Change the Text property from button1 to Say Hello.

The interface design is completed (see Figure 1-8). We now need to add code that will execute when the user clicks on the Say Hello button. Visual C# Express has been very busy behind the scenes—it has already written all of the C# code to generate the interface. All we need to do is write some event-specific code that will run when the button is clicked. This is known as an onClick event. We will use Visual C# Express to help us write the code to respond to the onClick event of our Say Hello button. Visual C# certainly makes life easy for a beginner. What would you do without it? I bet you can appreciate the advantages it has over Notepad now.

18. Double-click on the Say Hello button. The C# code for your application is displayed.

Notice that curly braces are used a lot. Don't worry if it looks a bit complex, because it will all make sense soon enough. The cursor is indented and placed within a method called button1_Click. This method will be executed when a user clicks on our Say Hello button. The Say Hello button is still called button1. We only changed the label of the button when we changed the Text property. The button and all other form controls have a Name property. We will now add some code.

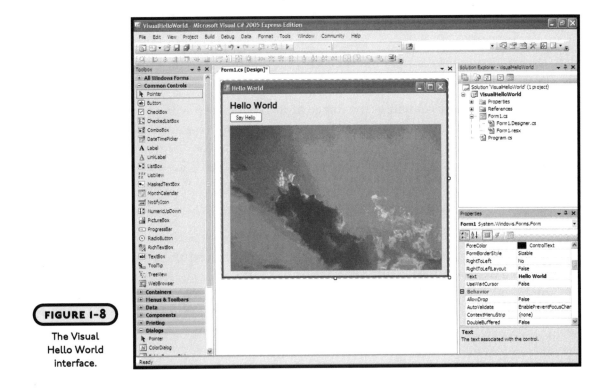

FIGURE 1-8

The Visual
Hello World
interface.

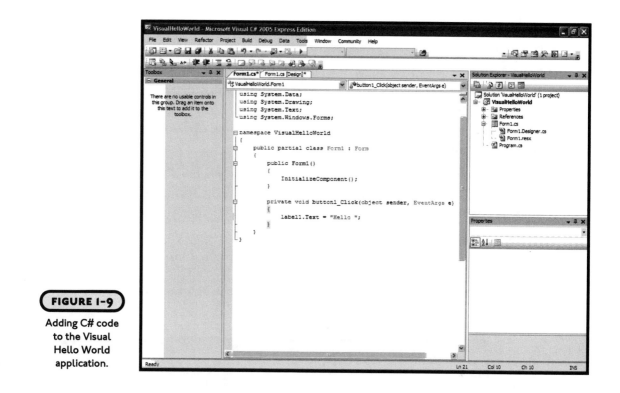

FIGURE 1-9

Adding C# code
to the Visual
Hello World
application.

19. Type your first line of code as shown in Figure 1-9: label1.Text = "Hello ";. The following is a description of the parts of this line:

label1 is the Label control, which currently displays the "Hello World!" text because that is what we previously set as its Text property.

Placing a period (.) between the name of the control and the property changes the Text property via code.

The equal sign (=) is an assignment operator. It assigns the value on its right to the property on its left. In this case, we want to change the Text property to say "Hello," followed by "the user's name." "Hello" is a string or a group of letters and must be enclosed in quotation marks so that it does not get mistaken for C# code syntax. A space is included after "Hello" because we are eventually going to add the name of the user to the end of the string.

Finally, the C# code statement must end with a semicolon (;). The semicolon tells the compiler that the line of code is complete.

We still have a bit of code to write, but it's a good time to test our application.

20 Click the Start button, represented by a Play icon on the toolbar. The C# Windows application will compile and launch.

The Hello World form floats above Visual C# Express, displaying the "Hello World!" text, the image, and the Say Hello button (see Figure 1-10). Clicking on the button changes "Hello World" to "Hello." You can also drag the form around the screen as well as resize it—just like any other Windows application. Click on the X in the upper-right corner to close the application.

Let's add a touch of personalization to the application. We need to get the user to enter his name. To do so, we will place an input box on the form and direct the user to enter his name.

21. Click on the Form1.cs[Design] tab. The Windows Form Design View is displayed again.

22. Drag a TextBox control onto the form.

23. Change the Text property to **Please enter your name** (see Figure 1-11).

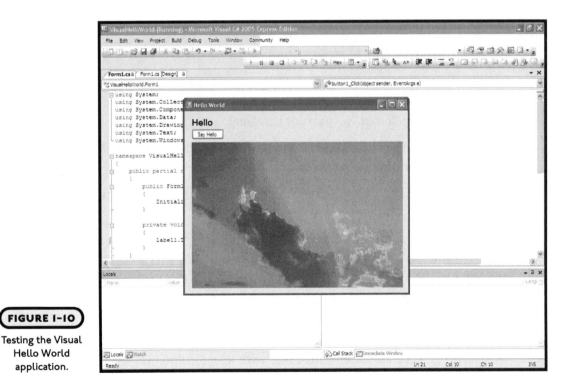

FIGURE 1-10

Testing the Visual
Hello World
application.

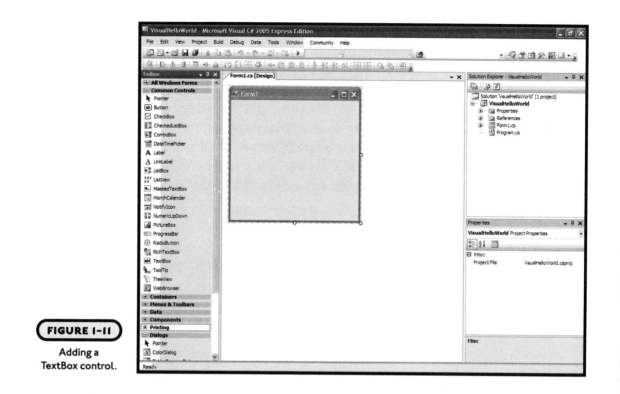

FIGURE 1-11

Adding a
TextBox control.

24. Double-click on the Say Hello button. This returns you to code view.

    We need to retrieve the text entered into the TextBox control and append it to the text that is assigned to the Label control.

25. Change `label1.Text = "Hello ";` to `label1.Text = "Hello " + textBox1.Text;`.

    textBox1 is the name of the TextBox control, and we can retrieve the name the user has entered from the Text property.

26. Click on File, Save All to save the project.

27. Click the Start button, represented by a Play icon on the toolbar. Test the Visual Hello World application.

You have just built your first fully functional application.

CREATING A CONSOLE HELLO WORLD APPLICATION

A program without a graphical user interface is known as a console application. A user interacts with a console application by entering text at a command prompt. Console applications existed in abundance before Microsoft Windows became popular. Console applications are still useful for complex processing tasks that require little or no user interaction. Most books on programming introduce a console-based "Hello World" application as the first programming example. It will be your second example program.

1. Click File, New Project to open the New Project dialog box.

2. Select Console Application as the project type.

3. Enter **ConsoleHelloWorld** as the application name in the Name field.

4. Click on OK.

   No Windows Form window is displayed after Visual C# Express creates the project, because you can't use interface elements such as buttons, labels, and text boxes in a console application. Instead, a panel in which you can enter your code is displayed.

   Visual C# Express has been busy behind the scenes again. It has written the C# code to create a console application. All we need to do is add some code to incorporate the functionality that we require. We'll need to add this code to the Main() method, which is executed when the console application is run.

   Our application only needs to write a line of text to the console. This seems pretty simple, but how do we go about doing this? We don't have any interface controls, such as a Label, and we can't simply set the Text property to Hello World. Fortunately, the Console class, which we can assess in a console application, has a method called WriteLine(). The WriteLine() method prints text to the console.

5. Type Console.WriteLine("Hello World!");.

   Pretty simple! "Hello World!" is passed to the WriteLine() method as a string (see Figure 1-12). This is a C# statement that calls a method. All statements must end with a semicolon (;).

6. Time to save the console application and then give it a good test. Click on File, Save All to save the project.

7. Click the Start button, represented by a Play icon on the toolbar. "Hello World!" will be displayed within the Visual C# Console window, as shown in Figure 1-13.

8. Press the Enter key to exit the program.

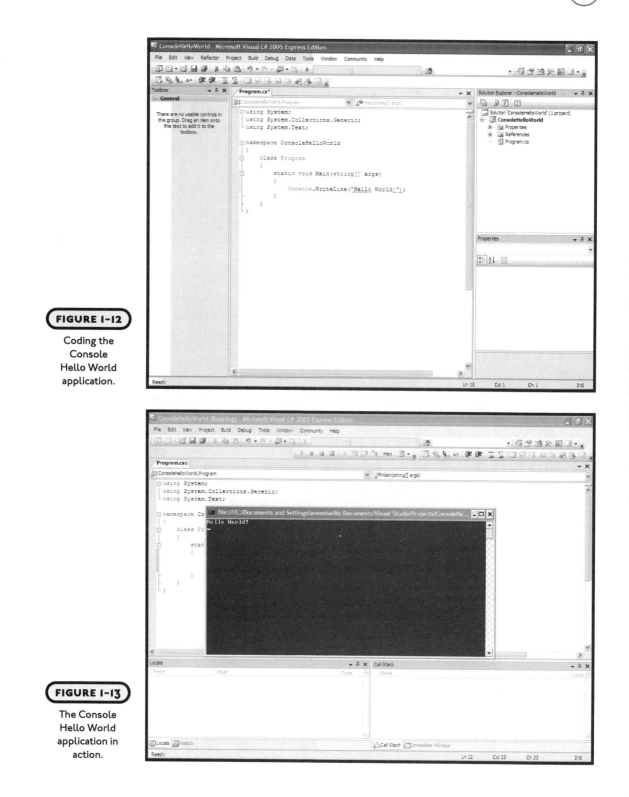

FIGURE 1-12

Coding the Console Hello World application.

FIGURE 1-13

The Console Hello World application in action.

BACK TO THE PICTURE VIEWER APPLICATION

The Picture Viewer expands upon the key concepts you learned while building the Windows Forms and console-based "Hello World" applications. The Picture Viewer is a Windows Forms application. The goal of this project is to illustrate that even beginners are capable of building intuitive and functional applications. It will also become evident as you progress through this example that Visual C# Express is the perfect companion for a beginner programmer.

The Picture Viewer is capable of displaying a variety of image file formats, such as GIFs, JPEGs, TIFFs, and BMPs. Users will also be able to use a dialog box to intuitively select the image they want to display.

Designing the Interface

Because the Picture Viewer is a Windows application (see Figure 1-14), we have at our disposal the full set of graphical interface controls available within the Toolbox. This means that we can build a fairly elaborate interface. It is a useful technique to sketch an interface before it is actually implemented.

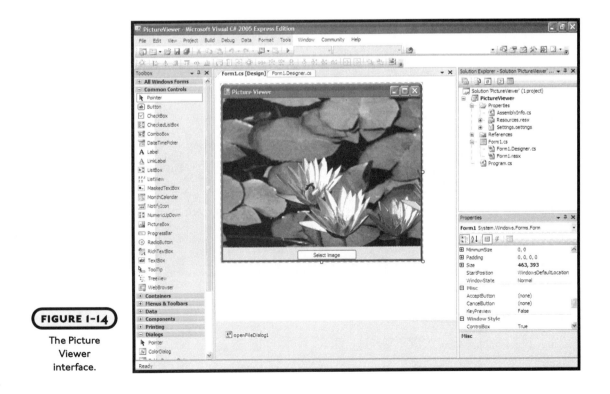

FIGURE 1-14

The Picture Viewer interface.

The Picture Viewer relies on the PictureBox control, which displays a variety of image types. We will also need a button that will open a dialog box. The user will use the standard Open dialog box to navigate to a folder and select the image that must be displayed.

Designing the Picture Viewer interface in Visual C# Express 2005:

1. Create a new Windows application called Picture Viewer.

2. Resize the default form within the Windows Form window.

3. Set the Text property of the form to Picture Viewer.

4. Drag a PictureBox control onto the form.

5. Resize the PictureBox control to match the size of the form. Leave some room for the button that will be used to open the dialog box.

6. Set the Image property of the PictureBox. This is the image that will be displayed when the application is first run.

7. Drag a Button control onto the form. This button will open a File Open dialog box.

8. Set the Text property of the button to Select Image.

9. Drag the OpenFileDialog control onto the form. The OpenFileDialog control is an invisible control. Instead, the OpenFileDialog icon is placed below the form, and it won't be opened until you write the appropriate code to perform this task.

Adding the C# Code

We now get to write the code that will turn the Picture Viewer into a functional application. The File Open dialog box needs to be displayed when the user clicks on the Select Image button. Thus, we need to place the code to trigger the dialog box in the button's onClick event handler.

How do we open the dialog box? An interesting question! We need to call the ShowDialog() method. After the user selects an image and then clicks on the OK button, the FileName property is returned. The FileName property contains the image name and path. We will need to assign this property to the Image property of the PictureBox control. This will display the image that the user has selected (see Figure 1-15).

1. Double-click on the button. The code panel is displayed, and you can start to enter your code.

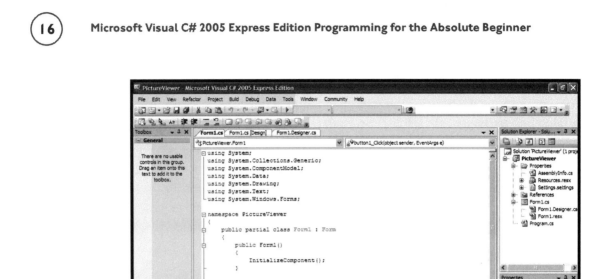

FIGURE 1-15

Coding the
Picture Viewer
application.

2. This code will display the dialog box. We use the if statement to test whether the OK button was clicked. We need to do this check because the dialog box also has a Cancel button:

```csharp
if (openFileDialog1.ShowDialog() == DialogResult.OK)
{

}
```

3. Type the following statement between the opening and closing braces of the if statement:

```csharp
pictureBox1.Image =Image.FromFile(openFileDialog1.FileName);
```

This line uses the PictureBox control to display the selected image.

Testing the Application

The final step involves giving our application a good test. Never underestimate the need for thorough testing. Testing is very important and essential if you want to deliver a fully functioning, bug-free application. The best way to test your application is to pretend to be the user—try out all the features and even purposely try to break the application. Test the application by trying to display different image types of varying sizes.

SUMMARY

You have made great progress and are well on your way to becoming an accomplished C# programmer. You have already programmed three applications, the final of which was a fully functional image viewer. You learned how to design a graphical user interface and add the C# code to make your applications work. You will use the basic techniques introduced in this chapter throughout the remainder of this book. Your C# knowledge will improve, and you'll be able to build more sophisticated applications and games. There are many exciting games waiting to be built in the remaining chapters, so read on.

CHALLENGES

1. Design a form to collect the name, e-mail address, and phone number of a user.

2. Make the console application output multiple lines of text.

3. Enhance the Picture Viewer by displaying the file name below the currently selected image.

C# BASICS

The C# language is intuitive, simple, elegant, and powerful. These features make C# the perfect language for beginners to learn how to program. After reading this chapter, you will feel comfortable with the C# language and programming. Key elements of the language such as statements, operators, expressions, and variables will be introduced. You'll also have a taste of problem solving, debugging, and writing documentation. In this chapter you will learn how to:

- Perform mathematic calculations.
- Debug syntax errors.
- Declare variables and constants.
- Write descriptive comments.
- Build a game to test your arithmetic skills.

PROJECT PREVIEW: MATH GAME

How good is your math? What is the sum of 33 and 105? Are you able to add 33 to 105 mentally? The Math Game, shown in Figure 2-1, is designed not only to put your mathematical ability to the test, but also to help you improve it. The Math Game can test your ability to add, subtract, and multiply numbers. Kids will enjoy playing the educational Math Game.

You start the game by specifying the type of math problems (addition, subtraction, or multiplication) you want to encounter in the game. You do so by selecting the appropriate radio button. The Math Game then displays a simple math problem that you must mentally calculate, as shown in Figure 2-2.

After you calculate the answer, you enter it in the blank field and click on Check Answer; then the game lets you know whether your answer is correct. Next, the game will generate a new math problem. You can play the game as long as you like—there are no time constraints. You can quit the game at any time by clicking on the X in the upper-right corner.

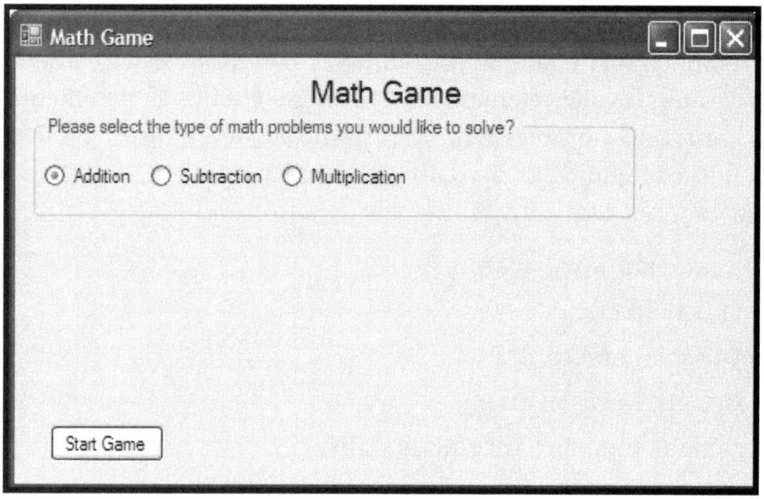

FIGURE 2-1

The Math Game.

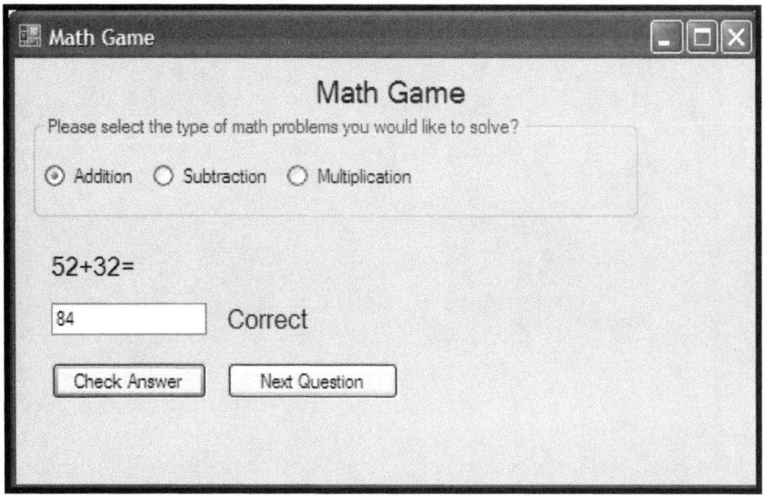

FIGURE 2-2

Playing the
Math Game.

C# Syntax

In the previous chapter, you had a quick look at C# code and even wrote a few lines of code. Writing code at first might seem a little cryptic (see Figure 2-3). This is true for all programming languages, including C#. It takes time to recognize C# statements and understand what the program is trying to do. The C# programming language is very structured, specific, and logical. It is made up of statements, expressions, operators, and variables. The same C# constructs are used in console-based and Windows applications. You'll learn a lot about C# syntax as this book progresses, but this section will help you to understand the basics.

The following line of code is called a statement. A statement performs a task and ends with a semicolon. All statements must end with a semicolon. If you forget to include a semicolon, your code won't compile. A semicolon is required so that the compiler knows that the end of instruction is reached.

```
Console.WriteLine("Hello World");
```

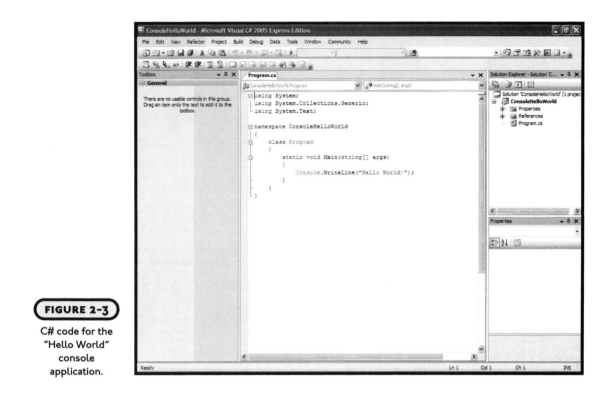

FIGURE 2-3

C# code for the "Hello World" console application.

C# code has lots of white space. Most of this code is generated by Visual C# Express. White space, such as blank spaces, tabs, and line and paragraph breaks, makes your code more readable. If you remove all the white space, your code will still compile, but maintaining it will be much harder. Visual C# Express automatically indents code as you type.

C# is case sensitive. This means that you must use the correct combination of upper- and lowercase characters. MyName, myName, myname, and MYNAME all refer to different variable names.

C# uses lots of parentheses. Both opening and closing curly braces are used and form matching pairs. Code within a set of matching opening and closing braces is called a block or code block. Essentially, braces group code. Opening and closing braces mark the start and end of the Main() method. In other words, everything included within the opening and closing braces is executed when the Main() method is run.

You'll also notice that method names are followed by opening and closing parentheses, such as Main(). WriteLine() is also a method, but we pass the "Hello World" string to it. The WriteLine() method takes a parameter.

DEBUGGING C# SYNTAX ERRORS

An essential skill for all programmers is the Ability to debug code. The debugging process involves locating and fixing errors in code. Syntax errors are the first type of error that you'll encounter. Syntax errors are usually the simplest type of error to fix.

Figure 2-4 shows a simple console application that is supposed to display the current time. However, it refuses to compile because it has several syntax errors (five to be exact), as described next.

First, notice at the bottom of Figure 2-4 that Visual C# Express displays an Error List window. If anything is listed in the Error List window, you won't be able to run the application. The Description column contains a short (and sometimes cryptic) description of the error. The corresponding line and column numbers help to locate the error within the code file. The Error List window displays four errors, but there are actually five errors in the code.

In the Description column, the first error says } expected. This means that we are missing either an opening or closing curly brace. If you look closely at the code, you'll notice that the Main() method has a parenthesis,), instead of a curly brace, }. Replace) with } to fix this error. This removes three errors from the Error List window.

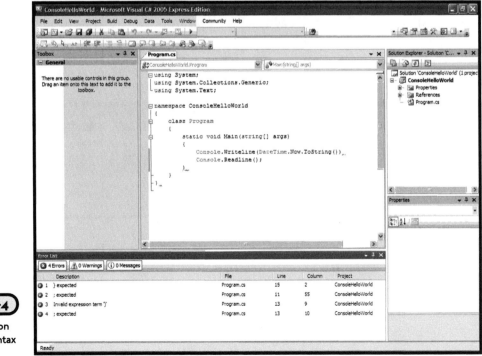

FIGURE 2-4

An application with many syntax errors.

The remaining error, ; expected, means that a statement in the code does not end with a semicolon. Find the statement and fix it. This clears the Error List window. If we have fixed only two of the five errors that the code contains, why is the Error List clear? The code still has errors, but Visual C# Express can't detect those errors without actually attempting to build the code.

Click on the Start toolbar button—it looks like the Play button on your VCR. Two build errors will be displayed. The first reads "System.Console does not contain a definition for Write-line." WriteLine() is a valid method that we've used before. Remember that C# is case sensitive. Writeline() and WriteLine() are actually different methods. Fix this error. Readline() also needs to be replaced by ReadLine().

Click on the Start button again. The code still has build errors because we have fixed only four of our five errors. The final error says that the code does not contain a Main() entry point. This means that we don't have a Main() method. We have another case-sensitive error to debug. We need to change main() to Main().

The code should finally run. Phew! Debugging is a time-consuming task and certainly requires a lot of patience. However, getting an application to work is very rewarding.

BASIC ARITHMETIC

C# excels at doing math. You can add, subtract, multiply, and divide numbers using a small set of operators, outlined in Table 2-1. You can place an operator between two numbers and C# will return the result.

TABLE 2-1 ARITHMETIC OPERATORS

Operator	Purpose	Example	Result
+	Addition	15 + 5	20
-	Subtraction	15 – 5	10
*	Multiplication	15 * 5	75
/	Division	10/5	2
%	Modulus	10/4	2

EXPRESSIONS AND OPERATOR PRECEDENCE

An expression is made up of a combination of arithmetic operators. When multiple operators are used, precedence follows the basic laws of arithmetic. Multiplication and division have a higher precedence and are performed before addition and subtraction. Expressions are also evaluated from left to right.

The following is an example of how C# evaluates expressions:

```
20 - 5 * 3 + 4/2
= 20 - 15 + 2        //Multiplication and division are performed first.
= 5 + 2
= 7
```

Use parentheses to change the order of precedence. Operations in parentheses are calculated first. The next example illustrates the use of parentheses to force addition and subtraction to be performed first:

```
(20 - 5) * (3 + 4)/2
= 15 * 7/2
= 15 * 3.5
= 52.5
```

VARIABLES

A variable associates a name with a value. This means that if you use a variable in an expression, C# will use its assigned value when performing the calculation. The value stored in a variable can be changed at any time. Variables are very powerful, and you will rarely build an application that does not use any.

There are many different types of data that you can store in a variable. Examples include text, numbers, and single characters, as outlined in Table 2-2.

Type	Example
TABLE 2-2 TYPES OF DATA STORED IN A VARIABLE	
Text	"Hello World"
Number	10000
Fraction	11.7
Character	'D'

C# is a strongly typed language, which means that when you create a variable, you need to explicitly define the type of data that the variable will store. This is known as *declaring* a variable. A variable that is declared as an integer can store only whole numbers. It cannot store text or even fractions. Refer to Table 2-3 for the list of numerical data types available in C#.

The following C# statement declares a variable called Name:

```
String VariableName;
```

The data type, string, precedes the name of the variable. A declaration is a statement and thus must end with a semicolon.

C# uses special keywords to define data types. The keyword in the preceding example is string, which is used to declare a variable that stores textual data.

You must abide by the following strict rules when naming variables:

- A variable name can't include spaces.
- C# reserved keywords can't be variables. Reserved keywords are part of the C# language and already have a purpose.
- Mathematical operators such as =, +, -, *, /, and % can't be used in a variable name.
- Variable names can't begin with a number. For example, 1Variable is an invalid name.

 TRICK Always give your variables descriptive and informative names. This will help when you need to debug and enhance your code in the future.

TABLE 2-3 C# NUMERICAL DATA TYPES

Type	Size in Bits	Range of Values
sbyte	8	–128 to 127
byte	8	0 to 255
short	16	–32,768 to 32,767
ushort	16	0 to 65,535
int	32	–2,147,483,648 to 2,147,483,647
uint	32	0 to 4,294,967,295
long	64	0 to 18,446,744,073,709,551,615
char	16	0 to 65,535
float	32	$1.5*10^{-45}$ to $3.4*10^{38}$ (7 digit precision)
double	64	$5.0*qo^{-324}$ to $1.7*10^{308}$ (15 digit precision)
decimal	128	$1.0*10^{-28}$ to $7.9*10^{28}$ (28 digit precision)

Declaring Whole Numbers and Fractions

Integers and floating-point numbers can be stored in a variable. The int keyword is used to declare an integer. An integer is a whole number, meaning it does not contain a fractional component. The float keyword is used to declare a variable that stores a number that has a fractional component, such as 5.234.

The following example demonstrates how to declare a whole number:

```
int Year = 2005;
```

A floating-point number is declared as follows:

```
float Age = 6.5;
```

In the preceding two examples, the variables are declared and then immediately assigned a value. The variables are declared and initialized in a single statement. The equal sign (=), or assignment operator, assigns the value on the right to the variable on the left. Here is an example that accomplishes the same task, but uses two statements:

```
int Year;
Year = 2005;
```

Multiple variables of the same type can be declared at the same time, as shown here:

```
int Year, Month, Day;
```

Once an integer variable is declared, we can store the result of a calculation within the variable. The following code creates a variable, assigns to the variable the result from adding two numbers together, and then outputs the variable to the console:

```
int sum;
sum = 5 + 20;
Console.WriteLine(sum);
```

We can also add together the values stored in a variable. In the next example, a number is assigned to two variables and then the two variables are added together. The result is stored in another variable, the contents of which are also output to the console.

```
int sum;
int no1 = 5;
int no2 = 20;
sum = no1 + no2;
Console.WriteLine(sum);
```

Strings

A string is a sequence of letters of the alphabet, numbers, and symbols (for example, !). A string could be a word or a sentence. String values are always enclosed within quotation marks.

The following is an example of declaring and initializing a string in a separate statement:

```
string Name;
Name = "Aneesha";
```

Declaring and initializing a string in a single statement is accomplished as follows:

```
string Name = "My name is Aneesha.";
```

And you can declare multiple strings at the same time in this manner:

```
String Name, Address, Country;
```

As you can see, the syntax to declare a string and the syntax to declare an integer are virtually identical. The only difference is that string values must be enclosed in quotation marks. The string keyword is used to declare a string variable. The equal sign (=) is also used to assign a value to the string variable.

Booleans

Boolean variables store only two values. Use a Boolean variable if the variable needs to store data that can be represented only in either of two states, such as true or false, yes or no, and 1 or 0. A Boolean variable is like a lamp, which can either be on or off. The `bool` keyword is used to declare a Boolean variable.

The following is an example of declaring a Boolean variable:

```
bool   IsValidUser;
```

Declaring and initializing a Boolean variable is accomplished as follows:

```
bool IsActive = True;
```

CONSTANTS

A constant, once set, contains a value that can't be changed. Constants are usually initialized at the beginning of a program and store configuration data. A value must be assigned to a constant when it is initialized. The `const` keyword is used to define a constant. In the next example, we defined a constant to store :

```
const float PI = 3.14;
```

WRITING DOCUMENTATION

Time spent writing documentation is time well spent. Comments allow you to insert small snippets of descriptive text with your code in a program. Comments are ignored by the C# compiler, but they are extremely important for programmers. You'll write many lines of code while learning to program and many more as an experienced programmer. A well-documented application is easier to debug, maintain, and enhance, especially if you are not the only programmer working on the project.

Documenting code is also good if you are in a position and you leave. The person that takes your place will be grateful.

There are two types of inline comments: single-line comments and multi-line comments. Inline comments can be placed anywhere within your code.

The following is an example of a single-line comment:

```
// This is a single-line comment
```

Everything from the start of the double slashes to the end of the line is ignored by the C# compiler.

A single-line comment can also be placed after a valid C# statement (remember that a statement ends with a semicolon) on the same line:

```
int x=4; //Declare an integer variable, x, and assign a value of 4 to it.
```

If you have a lengthy comment that spans more than one line, you can group together multiple single-line comments:

```
// Line 1 of a comment
// Line 2 of a comment
// Line 3 of a comment
```

However, a more efficient way to insert multiple lines of a lengthy comment is to use a multi-line comment. Anything placed between /* and */ is a multi-line comment:

```
/*
Line 1 of a comment
Line 2 of a comment
*/
```

The /* and */ symbols can also be used to temporarily stop sections of code from being executed.

The trouble with the previous two types of comments is that they can be found only by scrolling through lengthy scripts of code. C# has a third type of comment, not found in many other languages, that provides a way to structure and display documentation in an external HTML Web page. You still embed the comments in your code, but Visual C# Express is able to extract the data and then generate a Web page.

Documentation comments are very flexible. You can use XML tags to define different sections, all of which will be included on the generated Web page. Documentation comments are preceded by three slashes (////). Common XML tags include <summary> and <description>.

The following is an example of XML documentation embedded within a code segment:

```
///<summary>Brief one-line description of a method </summary>
///<remarks>Lengthier description of the method</remarks>
```

BACK TO THE MATH GAME

The Math Game is both fun and educational. It is also a challenging and ambitious programming project. You'll need to apply everything you've learned about graphical user interfaces and the C# language to complete the game. There are even a few concepts that you'll have to pick up while building the game.

Designing the Interface

The interface for the Math Game may look simple, but there is more to it than first meets the eye. We need to design the interface so that the Player can select the type of math questions and then click on the Start Game button. The Start Game button disappears, and the interface displays the Question field, the blank answer entry field, a Check Answer button, and a Next Question button. The Next Question button will allow the user to move through the game. This is also the first time we are going to use radio buttons. The Player will be able to select a radio button to indicate whether or not he wants to be asked addition, subtraction, or multiplication math problems during the game.

Creating the interface in Visual C# Express 2005, please refer to Figure 2-5 to determine the placement of controls:

1. Create a new Windows application called MathGame (refer to Chapter 1 for instructions).

2. Change the Text property of the form to Math Game. This changes the text that is displayed on the title bar of the form.

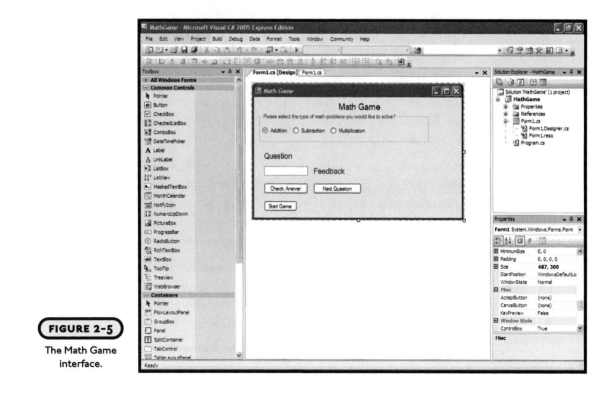

FIGURE 2-5

The Math Game interface.

3. Add and position a Label control at the top of the form. The label will display the game's title. Change the Text property of the Label to Math Game. Change the color and size of the text by adjusting the appropriate properties.

4. Drag a GroupBox control onto the form and position it below the title. The GroupBox control is located within the Containers section of the ToolBox. The group of radio buttons will be placed within the GroupBox. Set the Text property of the GroupBox control to Please select the type of math problems you would like to solve? This is the instruction to the user.

5. Drag three RadioButton controls onto the GroupBox control. Place the radio buttons beside each other. Set the Text properties of the radio buttons to Addition, Subtraction, and Multiplication, respectively. Set the Checked property of the Addition radio button to True, which sets the Addition radio button to be selected by default when the form loads. Placing all the radio buttons within a GroupBox means that only one radio button can be selected at a time. So, for example, if the Addition radio button is selected and then the user selects the Multiplication radio button, the Addition radio button is no longer selected.

6. Drag a Label control onto the form. This will display the math problem. Set both the Name property and the Text property to Question. This control does not need to be displayed when the form first loads, so set the Visible property to False. When the user clicks on the Start Game button, we will set the Visible property to True with C# code.

7. Drag a TextBox control onto the form. This is the answer entry field. Set the Name property to Answer. This control does not need to be displayed when the form first loads, so set the Visible property to False.

8. Drag a Label control onto the form and position it to the right of the TextBox control for the answer entry. This Label control will provide user feedback when the user clicks on the Check Answer button, so set both the Name property and Text property to Feedback. This control does not need to be displayed when the form first loads, so set the Visible property to False.

9. Drag a Button control onto the form and position it directly below the answer entry field. This is the Check Answer button, so set both the Name property to CheckAnswer and Text property to Check Answer. This control does not need to be displayed when the form first loads, so set the Visible property to False.

10. Drag a Button control onto the form and position it below the answer entry field. This is the Next Question button, so set the Name property to NextQuestion and Text property to Next Question. This control does not need to be displayed when the form first loads, so set the Visible property to False.

11. Drag a Button control onto the form and position it at the bottom of the form. This is the Start Game button, so set both the Name property to StartGame and Text property to Start Game.

Adding the C# Code

The main C# code in the game will be attached to the Check Answer, Next Question, and Start Game buttons. When the user clicks on the Start Game button, the button needs to disappear, and the interface needs to display the Question label, the Answer entry field (Answer TextBox control), the Feedback label, the Check Answer button, and the Next Question button.

To generate a math problem, we need to obtain two random numbers. You'll learn a lot more about random numbers in Chapter 5, but for now, here is some simple code that we can use in this application to generate random numbers between 1 and 100:

```
Random randomNo = new Random();
        int no1;
        int no2;
        no1 = randomNo.Next(100);
        no2 = randomNo.Next(100);
```

Writing the code for the Math Game:

1. Double-click on the Start Game button. The Code tab will be displayed. Enter the following code:

```
StartGame.Visible = false;
        CheckAnswer.Visible = true;
        Question.Visible = true;
        Answer.Visible = true;
        NextQuestion.Visible = true;
        Feedback.Visible = true;
        Gen_Question();
```

HINT Gen_Question() is a method that we will write later in this exercise. Its purpose is to generate the math problem and make the code reusable in a number of places in our code.

2. Scroll to the top of the file and, below the class declaration, enter the following code:

```
Random randomNo = new Random();
int no1;
int no2;
string problemType = "+";
```

These lines of code declare the variables that we'll be using.

3. After the closing brace of the StartGame_Clicked() method, enter the following code:

```
private void Gen_Question()
{
        no1 = randomNo.Next(100);
        no2 = randomNo.Next(100);

        if (radioButton1.Checked)
        {
                problemType = "+";
        }
        else if (radioButton2.Checked)
        {
                problemType = "-";
        }
        else if (radioButton3.Checked)
        {
                problemType = "*";
        }

        Question.Text = no1 + problemType + no2 + "=";
}
```

This code creates the Gen_Question() method. A random number is stored in no1 and no2. We then determine the type of math problem that must be generated. You'll learn much more about the if statement and decision making in Chapter 3. Finally, the method uses the Question label to display the math problem on the screen.

4. Click on the Form1.cs [Design] tab. The form will be displayed.

5. Double-click on the Check Answer button. Enter the following code:

```
int result=0;
if (problemType == "+")
{
        result = no1 + no2;
}
else if (problemType == "-")
{
        result = no1 - no2;
}
else if (problemType == "*")
{
        result = no1 * no2;
}

if (Answer.Text == result.ToString())
{
        Feedback.Text = "Correct";
}
else
{
        Feedback.Text = "Incorrect";
}
```

The answer is calculated and compared with the value entered by the user. The feedback given is either Correct or Incorrect.

6. Click on the Form1.cs [Design] tab. The form will be displayed.

7. Double-click on the Next Question button. Enter the following code:

```
Gen_Question();
Answer.Text = "";
Feedback.Text = "";
```

Here, we generate another question and clear the answer and feedback labels.

8. Write meaningful and descriptive comments for each method.

The full code listing for the Math Game:

```csharp
public partial class Form1 : Form
{
        Random randomNo = new Random();
        int no1;
        int no2;
        string problemType = "+";

        public Form1()
        {
                InitializeComponent();
        }

        private void StartGame_Click(object sender, EventArgs e)
        {
                StartGame.Visible = false;
                CheckAnswer.Visible = true;
                Question.Visible = true;
                Answer.Visible = true;
                NextQuestion.Visible = true;
                Feedback.Text = "";
                Feedback.Visible = true;
                Gen_Question();
        }

        private void Gen_Question()
        {
                no1 = randomNo.Next(100);
                no2 = randomNo.Next(100);

                if (radioButton1.Checked)
                {
                        problemType = "+";
                }
                else if (radioButton2.Checked)
                {
```

```
                problemType = "-";
        }
        else if (radioButton3.Checked)
        {
                problemType = "*";
        }

        Question.Text = no1 + problemType + no2 + "=";
}

private void CheckAnswer_Click(object sender, EventArgs e)
{
        int result = 0;
        if (problemType == "+")
        {
                result = no1 + no2;
        }
        else if (problemType == "-")
        {
                result = no1 - no2;
        }
        else if (problemType == "*")
        {
                result = no1 * no2;
        }

        if (Answer.Text == result.ToString())
        {
                Feedback.Text = "Correct";
        }
        else
        {
                Feedback.Text = "Incorrect";
        }

}
```

```csharp
private void NextQuestion_Click(object sender, EventArgs e)
{
        Gen_Question();
        Answer.Text = "";
        Feedback.Text = "";
}
```

TESTING THE APPLICATION

Spend a few minutes playing the game. Ensure that the Question label, answer entry field (Answer TextBox control), Feedback label, Check Answer button, and Next Question button are all hidden when the application starts. You might need the assistance of a calculator to be 100 percent certain that the game's calculations are accurate. Let family, friends, and kids play the game to ensure that it is fully functional.

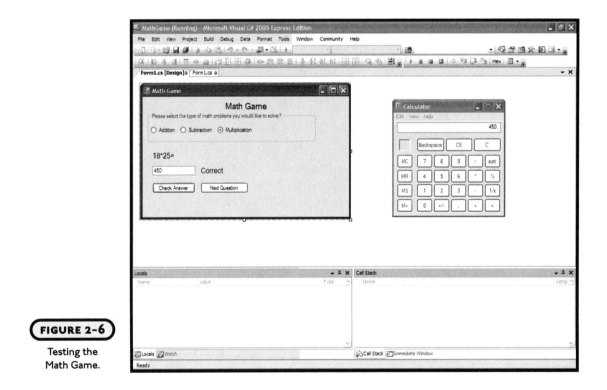

FIGURE 2-6

Testing the Math Game.

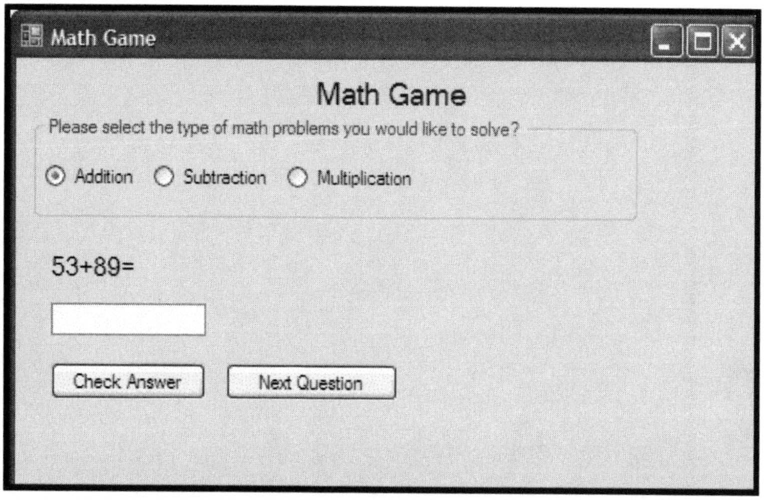

FIGURE 2-7

Generating an addition math problem.

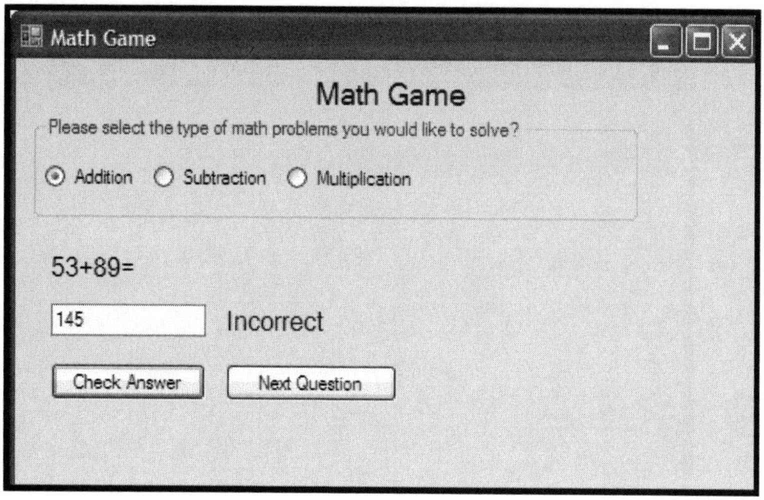

FIGURE 2-8

Checking if an answer is correct.

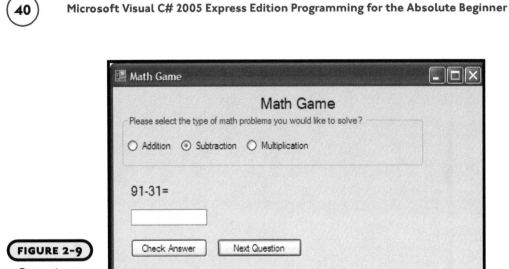

FIGURE 2-9

Generating an
subtraction
math problem.

FIGURE 2-10

Generating an
multiplication
math problem.

SUMMARY

You've learned a lot about the C# language and its syntax. Hopefully, C# no longer looks foreign to you. This chapter covered essential programming tasks such as debugging and writing comprehensive documentation. The core C# concepts introduced in this chapter, such as statements, operators, expressions, and variables, will be expanded upon through the remainder of this book and will be utilized in every application and game that you author.

CHALLENGES

1. A time limit on providing the correct answer to the math problem would certainly make the game more difficult. Add a 30-second time limit to the Math Game. You will need to use the Timer control.

2. Include an option that will randomly select the type of math problem (addition, subtraction, or multiplication) that must be generated.

3. Keep score—display the number of correct and incorrect responses in the Math Game.

CHAPTER

3

CONTROLLING
CODE FLOW

Every day you must make decisions based on varying circumstances. Similarly, your C# applications must be able to make decisions based on varying input. The C# code that you have thus far encountered in the previous two chapters has been very linear. We now focus on how to write C# code that is able to respond to dynamic and unpredictable events, such as a missing image file or the entry of incorrect information by a user. In C# we can evaluate expressions and decide which code needs to be run, which code needs to be skipped, and which code we need to execute multiple times. In this chapter you will learn how to:

- Use logical operators.
- Use comparison operators.
- Use if statements to make decisions.
- Repeat code execution with loops.
- Design and create a quiz.

PROJECT PREVIEW: THE SEESHARP QUIZ

The SeeSharp Quiz, shown in Figure 3-1, is a quiz that tests a user's knowledge of the C# programming language. The SeeSharp Quiz is a Windows Forms application. You need to use concepts introduced in Chapter 1, Chapter 2, and this chapter to implement this application. The concepts from Chapter 1 will help you to

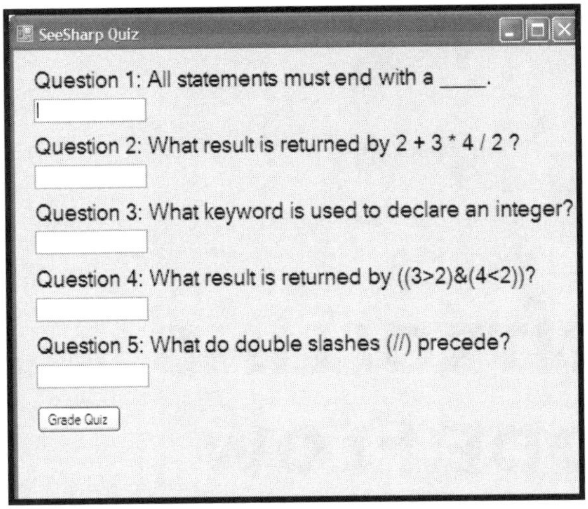

FIGURE 3-1

The SeeSharp Quiz.

design the interface. Chapter 2 concepts will help you to write C# code without syntax errors and store data in variables. In this chapter, you will learn how to grade the quiz.

The SeeSharp Quiz consists of five questions. All questions are displayed on one form. Users answer each question by entering text into a TextBox control. When the users have completed the quiz, they click a Grade Quiz button to see how well they did, as shown in Figure 3-2.

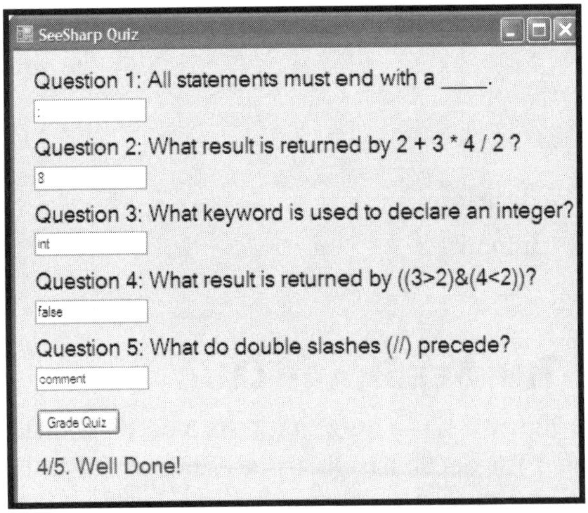

FIGURE 3-2

The graded SeeSharp Quiz. How well will you do?

Grading the quiz involves checking whether each answer is correct and then adding a mark to the user's total. We will need to do this for each question. Depending upon the score, we provide either flattering or encouraging feedback.

MAKING DECISIONS

The essential ingredient that is required to get the SeeSharp Quiz application up and running is to enable it to make decisions. The application needs to check whether the answer entered by the user is correct and, if it is, to increase the user's score. We also want the application to evaluate the user's total score when she has completed the quiz and provide appropriate feedback.

It is possible to write code that can intelligently respond to events that occur while an application is being executed. This ability to make decisions is extremely powerful, because it means that our code is not limited to a series of C# statements that are executed in a linear manner. Adding decision-making capabilities to code is the first step to making feature-rich, intelligent games and applications. It allows code segments to be executed after data has been analyzed.

Comparison Operators

Comparison operators compare data and return either a true or false result. Comparison operators can be used to compare strings, numbers, and even Booleans. You can use comparison operators to determine whether a value is greater than, less than, or equal to another value (see Table 3-1).

TABLE 3-1   COMPARISON OPERATORS

Comparison Operator	Meaning
==	is equal to
!=	not equal to
>	greater than
<	less than
>=	greater than or equal to
<=	less than or equal to

Let's take a look at some examples:

- ("Hello"=="Hello") returns a true value because the two strings being compared are equal.
- ("Hello"=="Goodbye") returns a false value because the two strings are not equal.
- ("Hello"!="Goodbye") returns a true value because the values are not equal and we are testing for inequality with the != operator.
- (5 > 3) returns a value of true because 5 is greater than 3.
- (3 < 10) returns a value of true because 3 is less than 10.
- (5 >= 2) returns a value of true because 5 is greater than 2.

Logical Operators

With logical operators, you can combine comparison results and create compound expressions. Put simply, this means that you can compare many values in a single statement. The logical operators, outlined in Table 3-2, include And (&&), Or (||), and Not (!). Each returns a Boolean value.

TABLE 3-2   LOGICAL OPERATORS

Operator	Description
&&	Returns a value of true if both values are true.
||	Returns a value of true if either value is true.
!	Inverts the true or false result.

The following are examples of the And (&&) operator, which returns true only if both values being evaluated are true:

- (True && True) returns a value of true.
- (True && False) returns a value of false.
- (False && True) returns a value of false.
- (False && False) returns a value of false.

The following are examples of the Or (||) operator, which returns true if either value being evaluated is true:

- (True || True) returns a value of true.
- (True || False) returns a value of true.
- (False || True) returns a value of true.
- (False || False) returns a value of false.

The Not (!) operator returns the opposite of the result being evaluated:

- !(True) returns a value of false.
- !(False) returns a value of true.

The if Statement

The if statement uses the result returned by a comparison or logical operator to determine whether the code should be executed (see Figure 3-3). The if statement is the key decision-making construct within the C# language. You will rarely program anything without using it.

The following is the basic syntax of the if statement:

```
if (expression)
{
// Code that is executed if the expression is true.
}
```

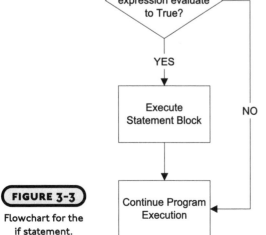

FIGURE 3-3

Flowchart for the
if statement.

The following is an example of using the if statement to decide what feedback a user should be given after taking a quiz. The feedback is determined by evaluating whether the user's score is greater than or equal to 15. Thus, we need to use the >= comparison operator.

```
if (quiz_score >= 15)
{
        result = "Well done! You certainly know your stuff.";
}
```

Some points to note about if statements in general:

- The expression that you are evaluating must always follow the if statement and be within parentheses.
- The expression must always return a Boolean value (for example, a true or false value).
- The code that must be executed if the expression evaluates to true is placed within curly braces.
- Multiple C# code statements can be placed within the curly braces that mark the start and end of the if statement.
- If the expression evaluates to false, the code within the curly braces is skipped.

The else Clause

The else clause adds to the if statement a code block that will be executed if the expression evaluates to false (see Figure 3-4).

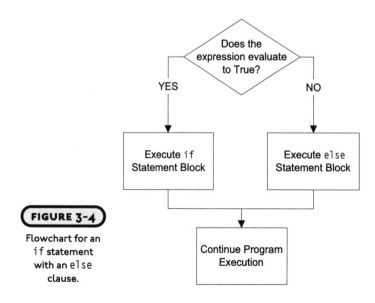

FIGURE 3-4

Flowchart for an if statement with an else clause.

The following is the syntax of an if statement with an else clause:

```
if (expression)
{
// Code that is executed if the expression is true.
}
else
{
// Code that is executed if the expression is false.
}
```

Some points to note about the else clause in general:

- The else keyword is placed after the closing curly brace of the if code block.
- No expression follows the else clause.
- The code that must be executed if the expression evaluates to false is placed within curly braces after the else keyword.
- Multiple C# code statements can be placed within the curly braces that mark the start and end of the else clause.
- If the expression evaluates to false, the code within the curly braces of the else clause will be executed. The code within the if statement will be skipped.

The else if Clause

The else if clause provides a way to evaluate additional expressions and execute the appropriate code if any of these expressions is true (see Figure 3-5). There is no limit to the number of else if clauses that can be included.

The following is the syntax of an if statement with else if clauses:

```
if (expression1)
{
            // code executed if expression1 is true
}
else if (expression2)
{
            // code executed if expression2 is true
}
else if (expression3)
{
            // code executed if expression3 is true
}
```

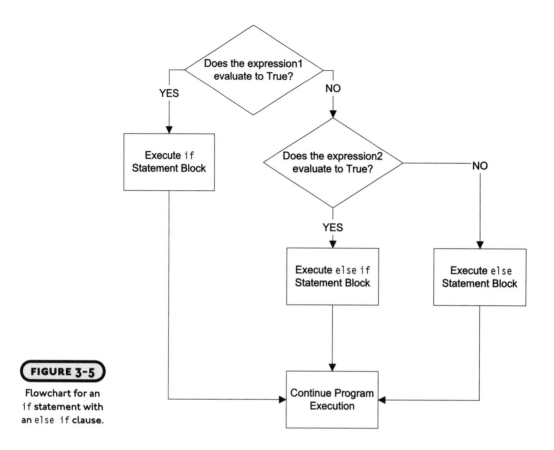

FIGURE 3-5

Flowchart for an
if statement with
an else if clause.

An else clause can also be included after a series of else if clauses. The else code block will execute if none of the expressions is true. The following is the syntax of an if statement with else and else if clauses:

```
if (expression1)
{
            // code executed if expression1 is true
}
else if (expression2)
{
            // code executed if expression2 is true
}
else if (expression3)
{
```

```
                // code executed if expression3 is true
}
else
{
                // code is executed if none of the expressions evaluate to true

}
```

We can now enhance the feedback provided by our quiz by using a series of else if clauses:

```
if (quiz_score >= 15)
{
                result = "Well done! You certainly know your stuff.";
}
else if (quiz_score >= 10)
{
result = "Not Bad! You know lots but could learn more.";
}
else if (quiz_score >= 5)
{
result = "Very bad! You need to study more.";
}
```

Some points to note about the else if clause in general:

- The else if keywords are placed after the closing curly brace of the if code block.
- An expression must follow the else if clause.
- The code that must be executed if the expression in an else if clause evaluates to true is placed within curly braces after the else if keywords.
- Multiple C# code statements can be placed within the curly braces that mark the start and end of the else if clause.
- If the expression evaluates to false, the code within the curly braces of the else if clause is not executed.
- The first else if clause that evaluates to true will be executed. All other else if clauses are skipped.
- If none of the else if clauses evaluates to true, all of the code in the if clause is skipped.

LOOPS

Loops repeat the execution of code blocks. Is this feature really required? Yes—loops are a very important part of the C# language. Let's say you had to calculate the amount an employee earns every two weeks. All you would need to do is write a series of C# statements to calculate. What if you had to perform this calculation for all the employees working in the company? Would it be practical to copy and modify the code for each employee? What if the company was extremely large and employed 50,000 people? A loop would allow you to write code to calculate the pay for an employee and then execute this code for each employee—50,000 times, if necessary.

The for Loop

The for loop is the most popular loop and is the preferred looping construct of many programmers. The for loop uses a counter variable to determine the number of times the code within the loop should be executed (see Figure 3-6). Each time the loop is executed, the counter must be incremented. When the counter variable reaches the required number, the for loop is exited.

The following is the syntax of a for loop:

```
for (initialize counter; check if counter equals the required amount of iterations;
increment counter)
{
            // execute code until expression is true
}
In the following example, the loop is repeated five times:
int i;
for (i=0;i<5;i++)
{
            Console.WriteLine(i);
}
```

Some points to note about for loops in general:

- The counter variable, i, must be declared before it can be used in the for loop.
- The counter variable, i, is initialized with a starting value.
- Each time the loop executes it is known as an iteration.

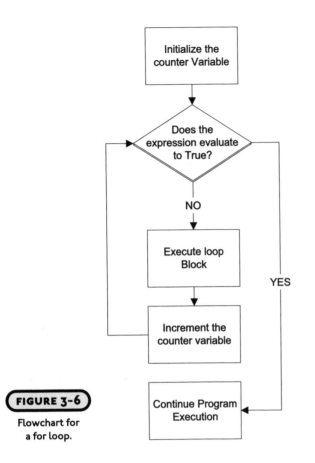

FIGURE 3-6

Flowchart for
a for loop.

- After each iteration, the expression (i<5) is evaluated. If this is not true, the counter is incremented (i++).
- Each loop control parameter is separated by a semicolon (;)
- All control parameters are placed within parentheses.
- Opening and closing curly braces mark the start and end of the code block that must be repeated.

A for loop simulation has been constructed to help you conceptualize how a for loop works. Open the interactiveforloop.htm file in a Web browser. You can change the for loop's parameters and see the effects these changes have on the output generated by the loop. Experimentation is the best way to learn.

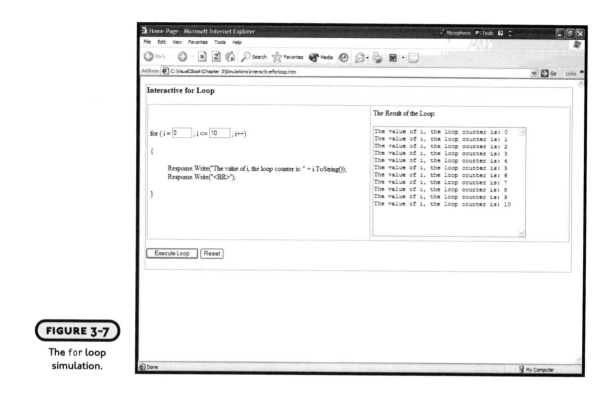

FIGURE 3-7

The for loop
simulation.

The while Loop

A counter is not required by a while loop. The while loop is executed until an expression eval-uates to true (see Figure 3-8). Use a while loop when you don't know how many times a loop should repeat, and you need your program to continuously perform a task until a condition is true. The syntax for a while loop is as follows:

```
while (expression)
{
                // execute code until expression is true
}
```

If you enjoyed using the for loop simulator, you are in luck because we also have a while loop simulator. Open the interactivewhileloop.htm file in a Web browser (see Figure 3-9). Adjust the settings to experiment with the loop.

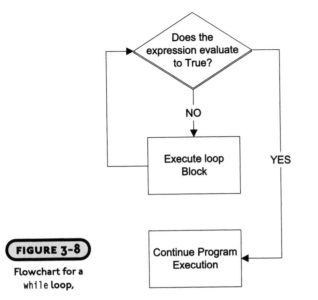

FIGURE 3-8

Flowchart for a
while loop,

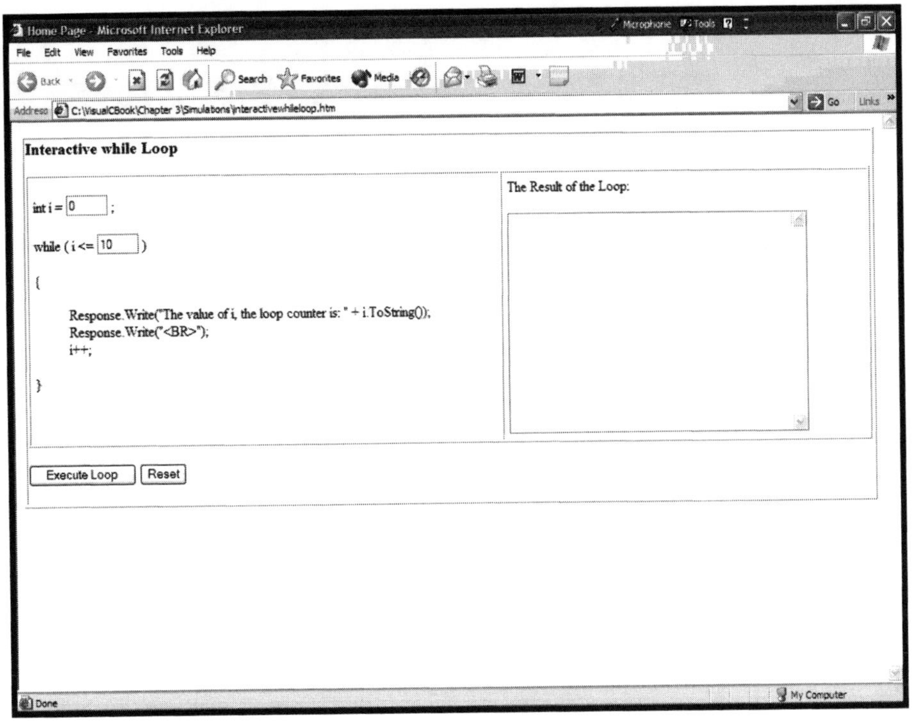

FIGURE 3-9

The while loop
simulation.

Exiting a Loop

There are two keywords that can be used to exit a loop if a condition is true. The `break` keyword terminates the loop and returns execution to the first C# code statement that follows the loop. The `continue` keyword stops only the current loop interaction. This means that the remaining code statements for the current iteration are ignored, and the next iteration is started.

The following is an example of using the `break` keyword to exit a loop:

```
for (i=0;i<5;i++)
{
            if (i==2)
            {
                break;
            }
}
```

Run the `breakSimulation.htm` file in a Web browser to experiment with using a `break` statement in a loop (see Figure 3-10).

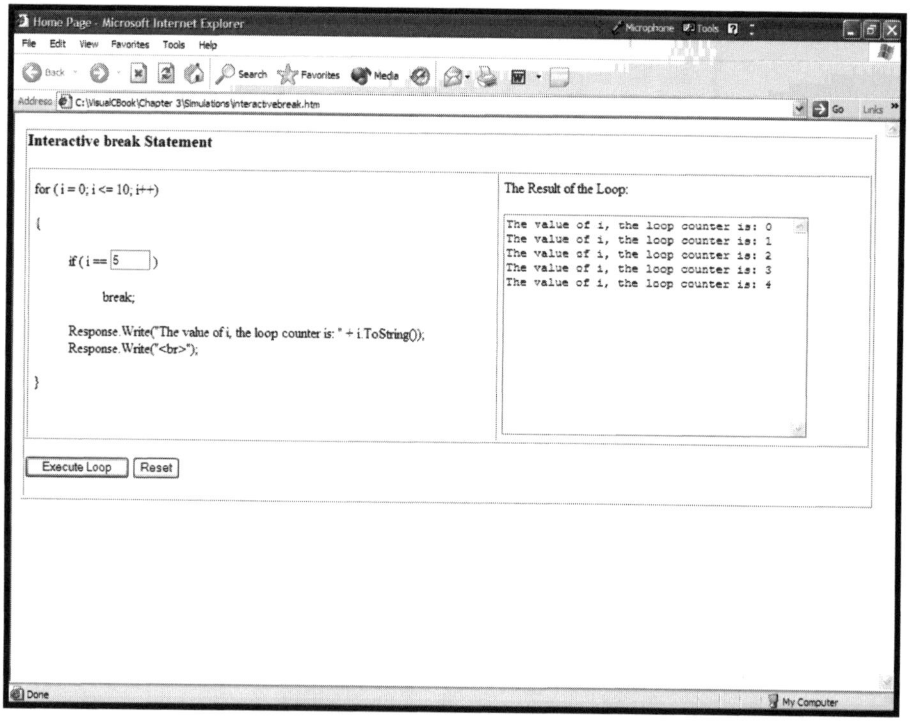

FIGURE 3-10

The break simulation.

An example of using the `continue` keyword to skip an iteration is shown next:

```
for (i=0;i<5;i++)
{
            if (i==2)
            {
                continue;
            }
}
```

Run the `continueSimulation.htm` file in a Web browser to skip a loop iteration with the `continue` statement (see Figure 3-11).

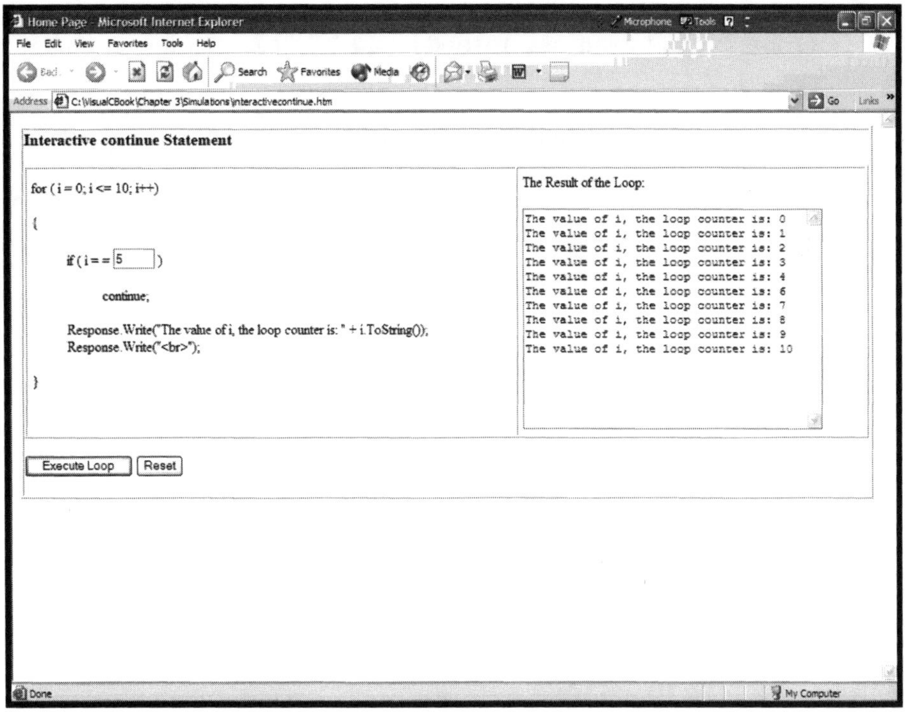

FIGURE 3-11

The `continue`
simulation.

BACK TO THE SEESHARP QUIZ APPLICATION

Equipped with an understanding of the if construct, we are now able to tackle the SeeSharp Quiz application. As stated at the beginning of the chapter, the SeeSharp Quiz tests the user's knowledge of the C# language. Our first task is come up with five really tough questions regarding C#. These questions may test anything covered in the first three chapters of this book. Our answers need to take into consideration all possible correct answers that a user can enter. Each correct answer is worth one point. The following are some examples of possible questions:

Question 1: All statements must end with a ____.

Answer: Semicolon (;).

Question 1 tests a fundamental syntax rule.

Question 2: What result is returned by 2 + 3 * 4 / 2 ?

Answer: 8.

The expression in Question 2 has no parentheses, so multiplication and division must be performed before addition and subtraction.

Question 3: What keyword is used to declare an integer?

Answer: The int keyword is used to declare integers.

Question 4: What result is returned by ((3>2)&&(4<2))?

Answer: False.

The And operator (&&) returns a true value only if both operands are true. They are not in Question 4, so a false result is returned.

Question 5: What do double slashes (//) precede?

Answer: Comments or comment or single-line comment.

Designing the Interface

The SeeSharp Quiz is a Windows Forms application (see Figure 3-12). This means that we'll be displaying the questions on a form. We will use Label controls to display the quiz title and questions, and include a TextBox control below each question. The user will be able to type answers into these TextBox controls. Finally, we need a Button control that users can click to check their responses, get feedback, and display the final quiz result.

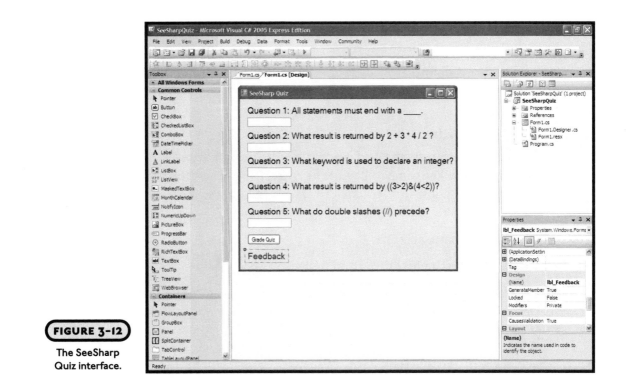

FIGURE 3-12

The SeeSharp
Quiz interface.

Design the SeeSharp Quiz interface:

1. Create a new Windows application called SeeSharpQuiz.

2. Increase the size of the form. The form needs to be fairly large to accommodate all five questions.

3. Change the text displayed on the title bar of the form by setting the Title property to SeeSharp Quiz.

4. Use Label controls to display the questions on the form. When laying out the form, remember to leave room for the answers between questions. Name the Label controls appropriately; e.g., lbl_Question1, lbl_Question2, lbl_Question3, lbl_Question4, and lbl_Question5. The Name property is used to set a label's name.

5. Add a TextBox control below each question. Answers will be entered into these TextBox controls. Give each TextBox control an appropriate name; e.g., Question1_Answer, Question2_Answer, Question3_Answer, Question4_Answer, and Question5_Answer.

6. Add a Button control to the form. Change the Button control's Text property to Grade Quiz.

7. Use Label controls to display feedback once the Grade Quiz button is clicked. Name the Label controls lbl_Feedback.

Adding the C# Code

The C# code to check each response and grade the quiz must be attached to the Grade Quiz button. Each response will be compared with the correct answer for the corresponding question. If it is correct, one point will be added to the overall quiz score. Feedback based upon the final grade will also be generated.

Programming the SeeSharp Quiz:

1. Double-click on the Grade Quiz button to display Code view.

2. Declare and initialize a variable called Grade, which will store the overall mark received by a user taking the quiz:

```
int Grade = 0;
```

3. Declare and initialize a variable called Feedback, which will be assigned feedback appropriate to the score received:

```
String Feedback = "";
```

4. Use an if statement to check if the answer entered in the Question1_Answer text box is correct. If it is correct, add 1 to the Grade variable. There are two possible solutions to this question, so we use the Or operator to check whether either solution has been entered.

```
if ((Question1_Answer.Text==";")||( Question1_Answer.Text=="semicolon"))

{
        Grade = Grade + 1;
}
```

5. Use if statements to check if the answers entered into the remaining text boxes are correct:

```
if ((Question2_Answer.Text=="8"))
{
```

```
                Grade = Grade + 1;
    }
    if ((Question3_Answer.Text=="int"))
    {
                Grade = Grade + 1;
    }
    if ((Question4_Answer.Text=="false"))
    {
                Grade = Grade + 1;
    }
    if ((Question5_Answer.Text=="comment")||( Question5_Answer.Text=="comments"))
    {
                Grade = Grade + 1;
    }
```

6. Next we need to determine the appropriate feedback that needs to be displayed. The if statement is used again:

```
if (Grade>=3)
{
            Feedback = "Well Done!";
}
else
{
            Feedback = "Could do much better!";
}
```

7. All that remains is to display the results. A message box will be used:

```
lbl_Feedback.Text = Grade +"/5. " + Feedback;
lbl_Feedback.Visible = true;
```

The full code listing for the SeeSharp Quiz:

```
public partial class Form1 : Form
{

    public Form1()
    {
        InitializeComponent();
    }

    private void button1_Click(object sender, EventArgs e)
    {
        int Grade = 0;
        String Feedback = "";

        if ((Question1_Answer.Text==";")||( Question1_Answer.Text=="semicolon"))
        {              Grade = Grade + 1;
            }
        if ((Question2_Answer.Text=="8"))
        {
            Grade = Grade + 1;
        }
        if ((Question3_Answer.Text=="int"))
        {
            Grade = Grade + 1;
        }
        if ((Question4_Answer.Text=="false"))
        {
            Grade = Grade + 1;
        }
        if ((Question1_Answer.Text=="comment")||( Question1_Answer.Text=="comments"))
        {
            Grade = Grade + 1;
        }

        if (Grade>=3)
```

```
    {
        Feedback = "Well Done!";
    }
    else
    {
        Feedback = "Could do much better!";
    }

    lbl_Feedback.Text = Grade +"/5. " + Feedback;
    lbl_Feedback.Visible = true;


    }
}
```

Testing the Application

Take the quiz yourself. Purposely enter incorrect answers and check that the grade corresponds accordingly. Questions 1 and 5 both have multiple correct answers. Try all possible combinations and ensure that the correct grade is calculated. You may also want to get a programmer friend to take the quiz, to see how it functions when taken by someone who did not create it.

Have you found any errors? You likely have—any answers entered that contain capital letters are marked incorrectly, because the responses are compared to all lowercase answers. To fix this bug, we need to convert the user's answers to all lowercase. In Chapter 5, you'll learn how to change the capitalization of strings.

SUMMARY

Two very important elements of the C# language were introduced in this chapter. The if statement is a powerful decision-making construct that will be used in almost all of the applications and games constructed in this book. The if statement, in conjunction with logical and comparison operators, enables the implementation of complex branching functionality. The other important programming construct introduced in this chapter is the for loop, which is able to repeat the execution of a code block a specific number of times.

CHALLENGES

1. Create a quiz on a subject of your choice. Your quiz could be on anything from music to ancient history.

2. Include pictures in your quiz. You will need to use the PictureBox control.

3. Provide detailed feedback for each question that a user answers incorrectly.

4. Include next to each question a button that the user can click on to receive clues.

5. Use a timer to limit the amount of time a user can take to answer the questions.

DESIGNING A USER INTERFACE

A well-designed interface enhances the usability of an application. The purpose of a graphical user interface (GUI) is to make a software application easier to use, explore, and navigate. We have a wide variety of GUI elements at our disposal, including buttons, labels, text boxes, radio buttons, check boxes, list boxes, and combo boxes. In Visual C# 2005 Express Edition, designing a complex interface involves no more than dragging controls onto a form. Interface design has never been easier. In this chapter you will learn how to:

- Design and customize forms.
- Add interface controls to a form.
- Align controls on a form.
- Use text boxes, check boxes, radio buttons, list boxes, and combo boxes.
- Design and program the Online Psychiatrist application.

PROJECT PREVIEW: THE ONLINE PSYCHIATRIST

In this chapter, we are going to do something slightly different by building an online psychiatrist. This is your first attempt at programming a computer program that is able to hold a conversation. It will involve some tricky C# code coupled with a very simple, yet intuitive, interface (see Figure 4-1).

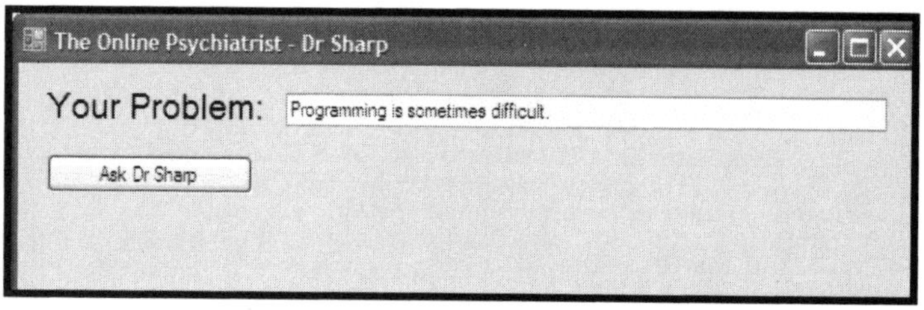

FIGURE 4-1

The Online
Psychiatrist.

The Online Psychiatrist, called Dr Sharp, is available 24 hours a day for a chat. Dr Sharp simply rephrases text that is entered by a user (see Figure 4-2). This application uses C# string processing techniques. This project will certainly amuse friends and family members. In this chapter, we'll also learn about interface design and Windows Forms controls.

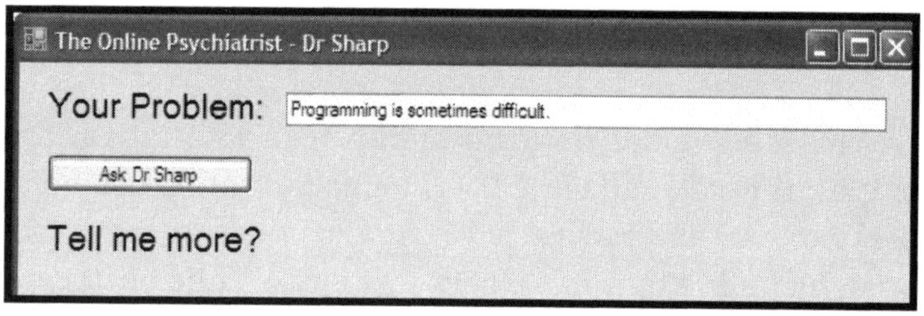

FIGURE 4-2

Chatting with
Dr Sharp.

DESIGNING FORMS

A form contains interface elements that convey information and encourage user interaction. Anything that you can view on a computer screen can be placed on a form and therefore be included in your application or game. Visual C# Express includes many interface elements (also known as controls), such as labels, buttons, toolbars, menus, tabs, dialog boxes, check boxes, and radio buttons, that you can simply drag onto a form from the Toolbox (see Figure 4-3).

When you create a new Windows application, a default form called Form1 is added to the application. Form1 is launched when the application is run. There are many ways that you can customize a form. For example, you can use the Properties window to customize a form. Press F1 with a property selected for help on that property. The first helpful thing that you can do is change the Name property of the form to something more descriptive (see Figure 4-4).

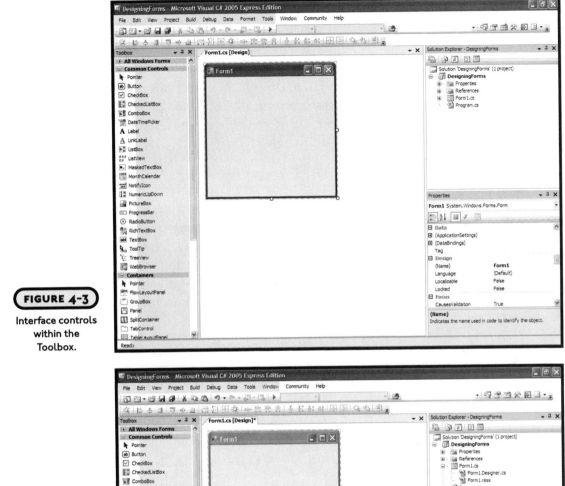

FIGURE 4-3

Interface controls within the Toolbox.

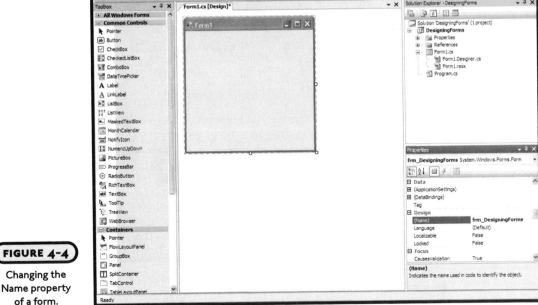

FIGURE 4-4

Changing the Name property of a form.

Next, you can change the Text property of a form, which is displayed on the title bar. The Text property helps a user identify the application. It could be set to the name of the application or to a description of the purpose of the form if multiple forms are used in the application. In Figure 4-5, we have set the Text property to Online Psychiatrist.

Forms by default have a gray background. All interface controls are gray in color. We can change the background color of a form by setting its BackColor property. Click the drop-down arrow to select a new color from a list of available system colors. Figure 4-6 shows a form with its background color set to Red.

You can also place an image on the background of a form. All controls will be drawn on top of the background image. The BackgroundImage property has a button with three dots—this is known as a build button. Click on this button to select an image. If the image is smaller than the form, it will be tiled or repeated. It is important to make sure that the text placed on a form can be read easily over the background image. In other words, you do not want to place red text on a background image with lots of red in it. Once you have set the BackgroundImage property, read-only subproperties become available. You can view these properties by clicking on the small box that contains a plus sign. Figure 4-7 shows the subproperties of the image.

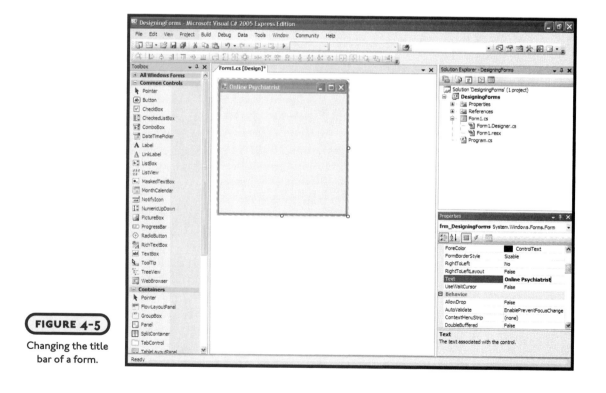

FIGURE 4-5

Changing the title bar of a form.

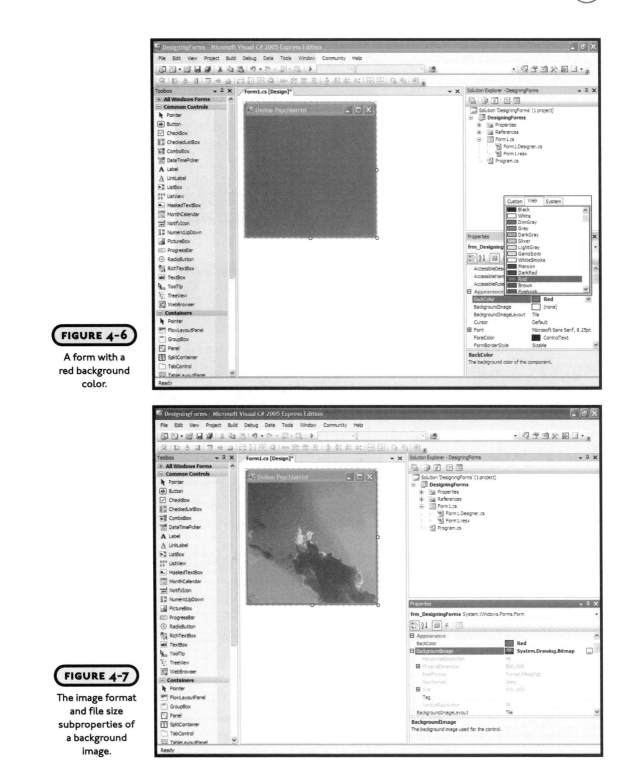

FIGURE 4-6

A form with a
red background
color.

FIGURE 4-7

The image format
and file size
subproperties of
a background
image.

You can use the Icon property, shown further down in the Properties window, to create a custom icon, a small image that is placed on the left side of a form's title bar. The icon is also displayed on the Taskbar when the form is minimized. If no icon is specified, a default one is specified by Visual C# Express.

You can also set the left and right coordinates for the initial display of a form, by using the StartPosition property. Table 4-1 contains the other display positions that can be set for the StartPosition property.

TABLE 4-1 FORM DISPLAY POSITIONS	
Setting	**Description**
StartPosition	Manual x and y coordinates specified in location property.
CenterScreen	Form is centered on computer monitor.
WindowsDefaultLocation	Form is placed in upper-left corner.
WindowsDefaultBound	Form is placed in upper-left corner and the size of the form is set to the screens bounds.
CenterParent	Form is centered within the parent window.

ADDING CONTROLS TO A FORM

Interface controls that can be added to a form are found in the Toolbox docked window on the left side of the Visual C# Express interface. Controls are categorized within panels. Click on a panel to display a specific set of controls. We will mostly be using the Common Controls panel, shown in Figure 4-8.

There are three ways that you can add a control to a form:

- **Double-click on a control.** This adds the control to the upper-left corner of the form. You can then manually drag the control to a new position on the form.
- **Drag a control onto the form.** This places the control at an exact position.
- **Draw a control on the form.** This sounds a little tricky, but it is really quite simple. First, select the control by clicking on it within the Toolbox window. Then use the mouse to draw a box on the form. When you release the mouse button, the selected control will be added to the form with the dimensions of the box. This method is very useful if you want to add a control with a specific size.

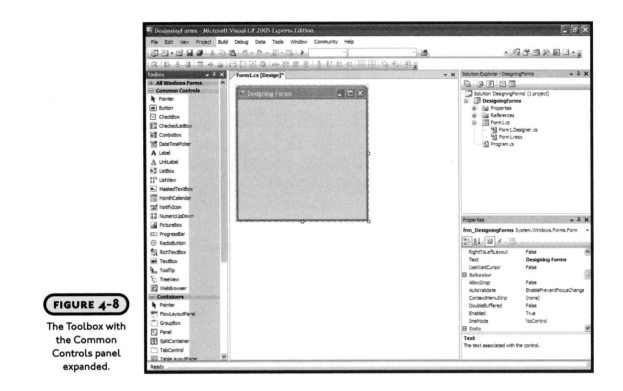

FIGURE 4-8

The Toolbox with
the Common
Controls panel
expanded.

Visual C# Express uses grids in form design view. The grid helps us to position controls. Controls snap to grid points, which makes it easier to position and align multiple controls.

SELECTING A GROUP OF CONTROLS

Aligning multiple controls on a form individually can be a time-consuming task. Fortunately, Visual C# Express provides a way to select multiple controls and perform various functions on them collectively, including aligning and spacing them and setting their properties.

Once a control is selected, the previously selected control gets deselected. There are two ways to select multiple controls on a form:

- **Lasso the controls.** This entails using the mouse to draw a box of the controls that need to be selected. All controls that intersect the mouse-drawn box are selected.
- **Use Shift+click.** Hold down the Shift key while using the mouse to click on and select multiple controls.

The control with black centered sizing handles is known as the active control (see Figure 4-9). When attributes of the active control are changed, these changes are inherited by all other controls in the group.

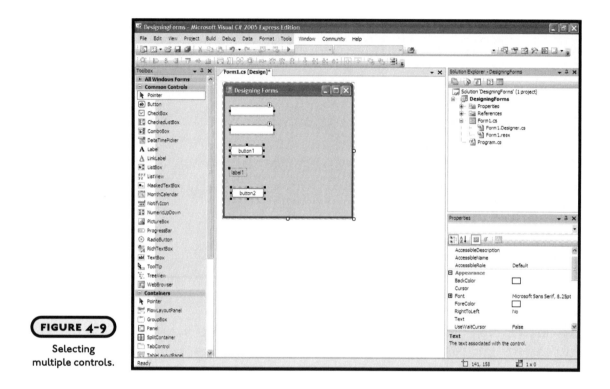

FIGURE 4-9

Selecting multiple controls.

Aligning and Spacing Controls

Alignment tools are found on the Format menu, under Align, shown in Figure 4-10. The alignment options can be applied to either a single control or multiple controls. When alignment options are applied to multiple controls, values from the active control are used.

We can also change the spacing between controls. As you can see in Figure 4-11, the Format menu also includes options for adjusting the vertical and horizontal space between controls.

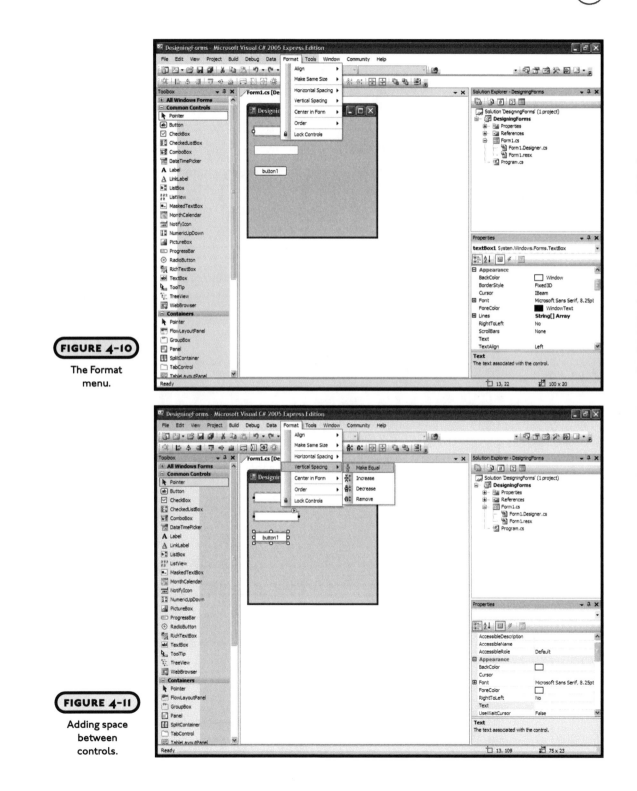

FIGURE 4-10

The Format menu.

FIGURE 4-11

Adding space between controls.

Setting Properties for Multiple Controls

The Properties window displays a reduced set of properties when multiple controls are selected (see Figure 4-12). Only common or shared properties are editable. The Name property, for example, must be unique and therefore can't be assigned to a group of controls. You'll also notice that some properties are blank, such as the Location property, which is blank because each control in the group has a different location.

As you can see in Figure 4-13, changing the BackColor property changes the color of all controls in the group.

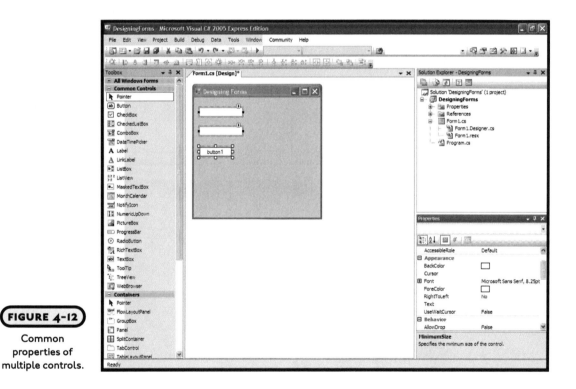

FIGURE 4-12

Common properties of multiple controls.

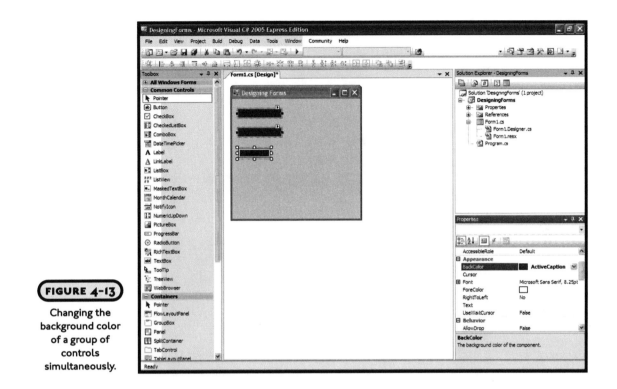

FIGURE 4-13

Changing the
background color
of a group of
controls
simultaneously.

LABEL CONTROL

The Label control is a very simple, yet fundamental control. The Label control displays text on a form. The Text property of the Label control contains the text that is displayed. You have full control over the positioning, font, font size, and color of the text that is displayed. Figure 4-14 shows Label controls being used on a form.

A user can't directly edit the Label control's text. The Label control is not designed to capture text entered by the user; its purpose is simply to display text. We can, however, modify the Text property from code. In this code snippet, we change the Text property for a Label control with a Name of label1:

```
label1.Text = "Hello - I am a Label Control";
```

FIGURE 4-14

Using the Label
control to
display text.

TextBox Control

The TextBox control allows users to enter text or edit existing text. We use the TextBox control to collect structured data from users, so that we can then write code to process and store the data. The form in Figure 4-15 has a TextBox control.

The TextBox controls in Figure 4-15 do not display text by default. We have to set the Text property to display an instruction or the data that a user needs to edit (see Figure 4-16).

If a TextBox control needs to display default text that the user can then edit, the default text must be assigned to the Text property of the control. We can also set the default text from code, as in the following example:

```
TextBox1.Text = "Hello - I am a TextBox Control";
```

It is also very easy to retrieve the data that a user has entered into a TextBox control:

```
String name = TextBox1.Text;
```

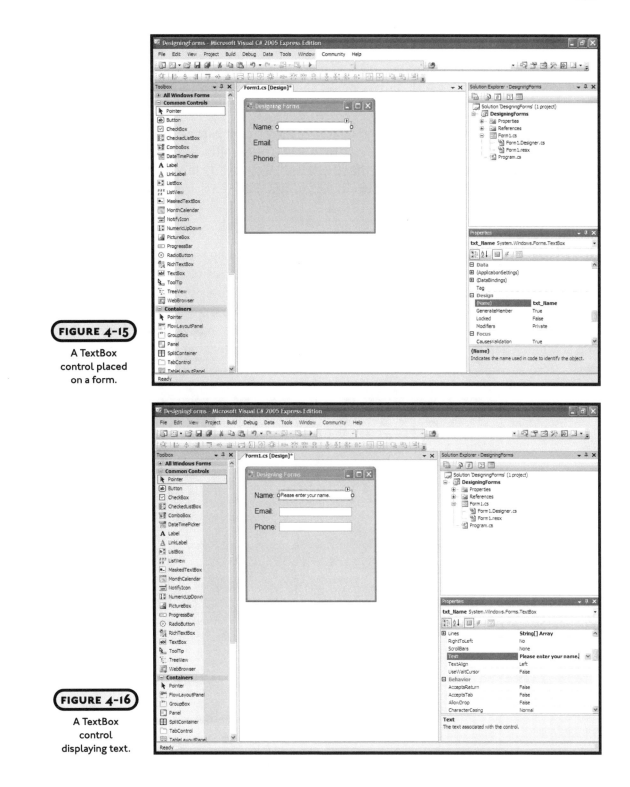

FIGURE 4-15

A TextBox
control placed
on a form.

FIGURE 4-16

A TextBox
control
displaying text.

MULTILINE TEXT BOXES

A TextBox control by default only allows a single line of text to be entered. We can only resize a TextBox control's width, unless we set the Multiline property to True, as shown in Figure 4-17.

Another useful property to set is the ScrollBars property. Scroll bars enable the user to enter more text than the dimensions of the control allow. The ScrollBars property can be set to None, Vertical, Horizontal, or Both. Setting the ScrollBars property to Both enables both vertical and horizontal scroll bars, as shown in Figure 4-18.

Entering a Password

We can easily turn any TextBox control into a password field by setting the PasswordChar property of the TextBox control to * (see Figure 4-19). Using an * is a standard convention, but we could set the PasswordChar property to any character. A password field captures and stores top-secret data entered by a user, but does not display it onscreen. This prevents somebody from looking over the shoulder of a user and stealing their password or other sensitive information. A password field displays an asterisk for each letter that a user enters.

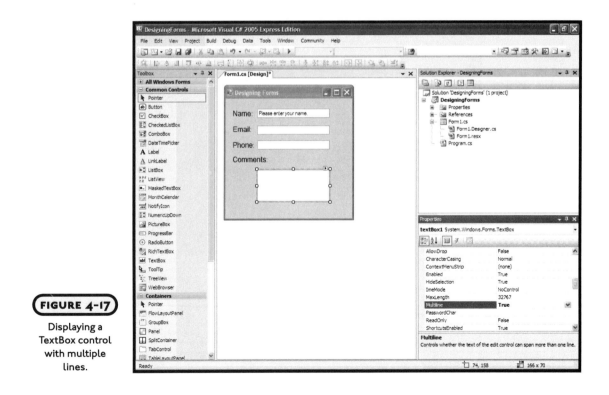

FIGURE 4-17

Displaying a TextBox control with multiple lines.

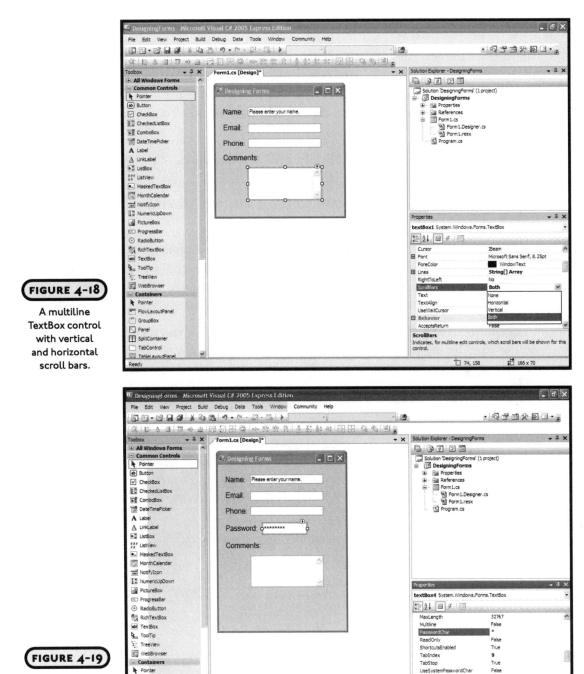

FIGURE 4-18

A multiline
TextBox control
with vertical
and horizontal
scroll bars.

FIGURE 4-19

A password field
displays an
asterisk for each
character entered
by a user.

Button Control

A Button control triggers the execution of C# code contained within a method. The text that is displayed on a Button control is set via its Text property. Let's build a simple Windows Forms application that contains a Label control and a Button control, as shown in Figure 4-20. When the user clicks on the Button control, the text that the Label control displays will change.

1. Create a new Windows Forms application called ButtonControl. This is explained in Chapter 1.

2. Change the Text property of the form to Using a Button. This changes the text that is displayed on the title bar of the form.

3. Add and position a Label control at the top of the form. The label will display an initial text statement. Change the Text property of the Label control to Some text that will be changed when the button is clicked. Change the color and size of the text by adjusting the appropriate properties.

4. Drag a Button control onto the form and position it below the text entry field. This will be the Change Text button.

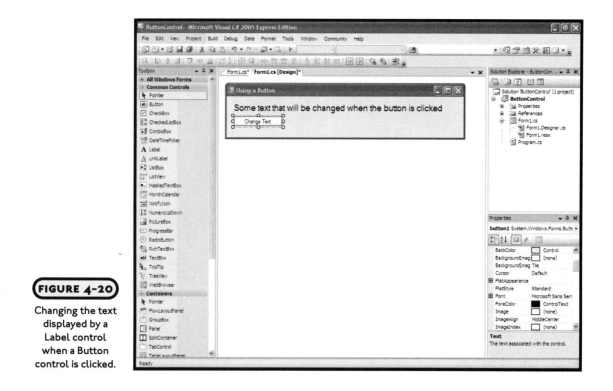

FIGURE 4-20

Changing the text displayed by a Label control when a Button control is clicked.

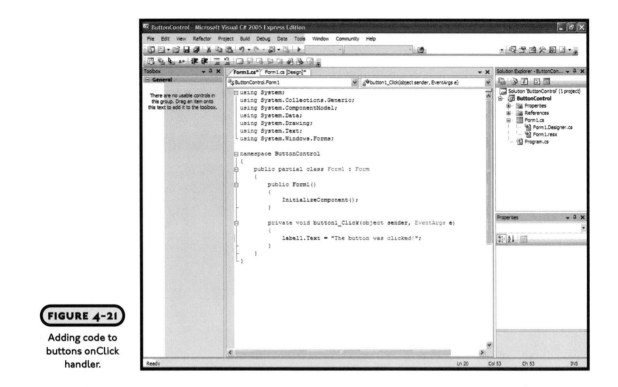

FIGURE 4-21

Adding code to
buttons onClick
handler.

5. Double-click on the Change Text button. The Form1.cs tab will be displayed (see Figure 4-21). Enter the following code within the button's onClick handler:

```
label1.Text = "The button was clicked!";
```

6. Click on the Start button to run the program.

7. Click on the Change Text button. The text displayed by the Label control will change (see Figure 4-22).

FIGURE 4-22

Clicking on the
Change Text
button.

GroupBox Control

A GroupBox control is a container control—this means that other controls can be placed within a GroupBox control. A GroupBox control has a frame-like border and a caption (see Figure 4-23). Related controls are usually dragged onto a GroupBox control.

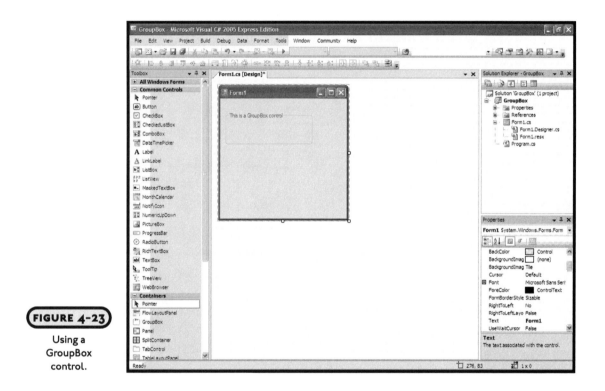

FIGURE 4-23

Using a GroupBox control.

CheckBox Control

A CheckBox control (see Figure 4-24) is a square control that is either checked (has a tick inside its box) or unchecked. The state of the CheckBox control changes when a user clicks on the corresponding check box. CheckBox controls store yes/no or true/false data. They are useful when you need to present a series of Yes/No options to a user. Setting the Checked property to True, checks the CheckBox when the form loads.

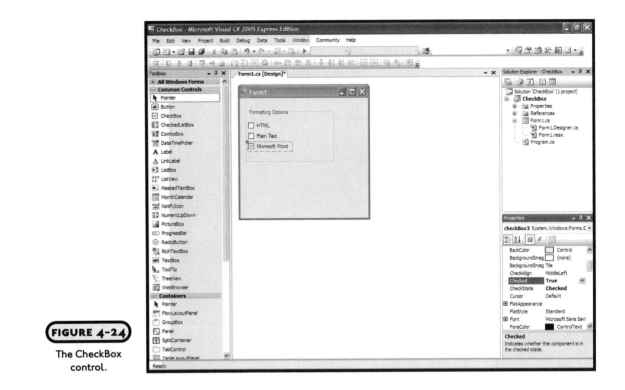

FIGURE 4-24

The CheckBox
control.

[Checking the status of a CheckBox from code:

```
if (checkBox1.Checked)
{
      // if checkBox1.Checked is true so this code block is executed
      label1.Text = "checkBox1 is checked";
}
```

RADIOBUTTON CONTROL

RadioButton controls are round in shape (see Figure 4-25) and are placed within a GroupBox control. RadioButton controls placed within a GroupBox control are mutually exclusive. This means that a set of RadioButton controls presents a series of options to the user, but the user can select only a single option. Selecting a radio button automatically deselects the previously selected radio button. We can specify the radio button that is checked by default (when a form loads) by setting its Checked property to True.

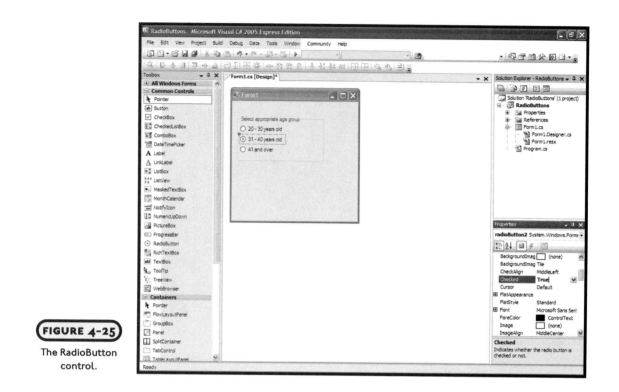

FIGURE 4-25

The RadioButton
control.

Checking if a RadioButton is selected from code:

```
if (radioButton1.Checked)
{
    // if radioButton1.Checked is true so this code block is executed
    label1.Text = "radioButton1 is selected";
}
```

LISTBOX CONTROL

A ListBox control displays items in a list, as shown in Figure 4-26. A user can select a single item or multiple items from a list. A ListBox control can even have scroll bars, if the items can't all be displayed within the control's dimensions.

We can add items to the list by clicking on the Build button located within the Items Collection property. This displays the String Collection Editor, in which we can enter items into the text box one line at a time (see Figure 4-27).

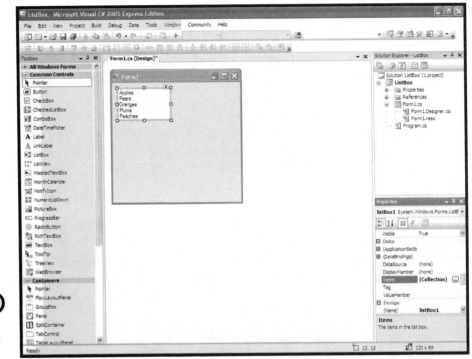

FIGURE 4-26

Displaying a list of items within a ListBox control.

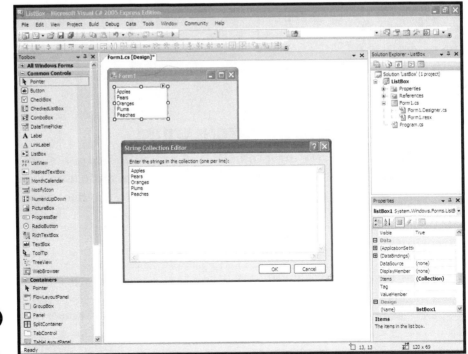

FIGURE 4-27

The String Collection Editor.

We can also add items to a ListBox control with C# code, as in this example:

```
int intIndex;
intIndex = lstListCtrl.Items.Add("new Item");
We can also remove an item from a list:
lstListCtrl.Items.Remove("new Item");
The item that a user has selected can be retrieved as follows:
int selectedItemIndex = lstListCtrl.SelectedIdex;
string selectedItem  = lstListCtrl.SelectedItem;
```

ComboBox Control

The ListBox control covered in the previous section has two shortcomings: it can take up a lot of screen space, and the user can't enter custom values. The ComboBox control solves these two problems. The ComboBox control has a button with a drop-down arrow that, when clicked on, displays a list of items that a user can select (see Figure 4-28). The user can also enter his own value.

FIGURE 4-28

The ComboBox control.

Back to the Online Psychiatrist

I'm sure that you are very eager to build the virtual Dr Sharp, the psychiatrist that will reside on your computer. Building the Online Psychiatrist program will utilize programming concepts covered in previous chapters, as well as the interface design techniques that you learned in this chapter. Let's start this exciting project.

Designing the Interface

Figure 4-29 illustrates the interface that our application will use. The interface only uses labels, text boxes, and a button. It is simple and intuitive, meaning even a novice computer user will be able to use it. To create the interface, follow these steps:

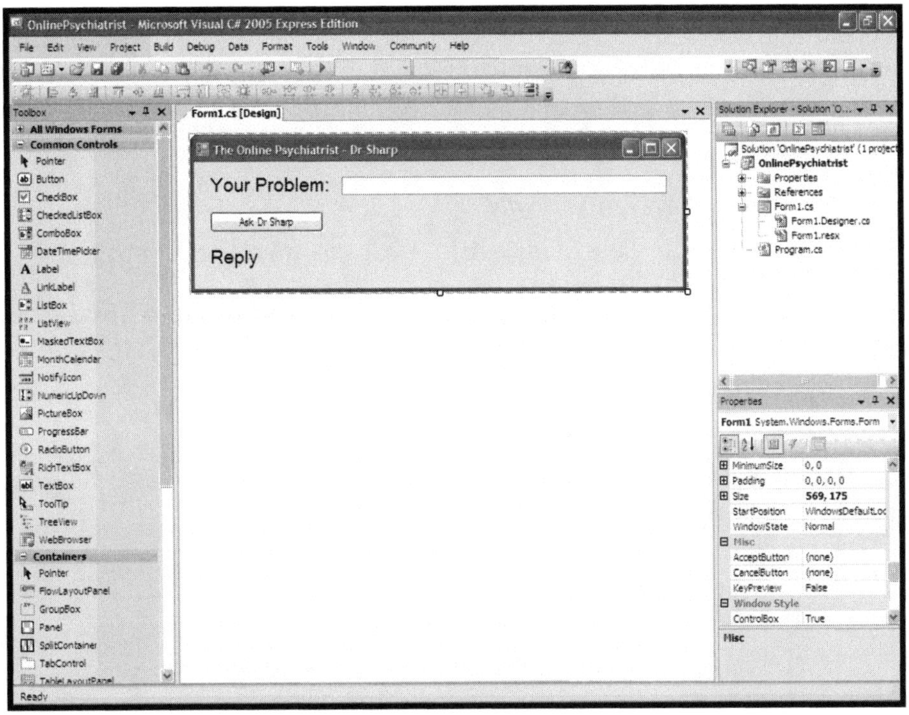

FIGURE 4-29

The Online
Psychiatrist.

1. Create a new Windows Forms application called OnlinePsychiatrist.

2. Change the Text property of the form to The Online Psychiatrist–Dr Sharp. This changes the text that is displayed on the title bar of the form.

3. Add and position a Label control at the top of the form. Change the Text property of the Label control to Your Problem:. Change the color and size of the text by adjusting the appropriate properties.

4. Drag a TextBox control onto the form. This is the text entry field. Set the Name property to Problem.

5. Drag a Button control onto the form and position it below the Your Problem label. Set the Text property to Ask Dr Sharp.

6. Drag a Label control onto the form and position it below the Button control. This label will initially be blank, but later will display Dr Sharp's reply. Set the Name property to Reply. Set the Visible property to False.

Programming the C# Code

Dr Sharp is able to chat by transforming and rephrasing the text entered by a user. The following are the three replies that Dr Sharp can randomly make:

- "Tell me more."
- "Have you always felt this way?"
- Replace "I" with "You," "am" with "are," and "my" with "your."

Double-click on the Ask Dr Sharp button. The Form1.cs tab will be displayed. Enter the following code:

```
String ReplyText;
Random randomNo = new Random();
int responseType = randomNo.Next(3);
if (responseType ==0)
{
        ReplyText = "Tell me more?";
}
else if (responseType ==1)
{
        ReplyText = "Have you always felt this way?";
}
else
{
        ReplyText = Problem.Text;
        ReplyText = ReplyText.Replace("I","You");
        ReplyText = ReplyText.Replace(" am "," are ");
        ReplyText = ReplyText.Replace(" my "," your ");
}
Reply.Text = ReplyText;
Reply.Visible = true;
```

Testing the Game

Time to test the Online Psychiatrist, or "visit Dr Sharp." You need to make sure that all three response types are returned. You also need to enter text that contains "I," "am," and "my" to ensure that these words are changed to "You," "are," and "your," respectively. Get friends and family to chat to Dr Sharp as well.

Summary

The importance of a well-designed interface can never be underestimated. Visual C# 2005 Express Edition makes it easy to design interfaces, but you still have to put some thought into selecting the appropriate control that matches the type of user interaction you are after. In this chapter, we have looked at the controls for labels, buttons, radio buttons, check boxes, list boxes, combo boxes, and group boxes. There are many more controls that you can use to add interface items, such as dialog boxes, tabs, menus, and toolbars. Don't worry because these will be covered in later chapters.

Challenges

1. Design a form that uses all of the interface controls covered in this chapter.

2. Build a Fahrenheit to Celsius temperature converter. You may need to use Google to do some research on the equation required to convert temperature from Fahrenheit to Celsius.

3. Write a program that has buttons to add, remove, and reorder items in a ListBox control.

4. Design and build a calculator using Button controls and a single Label control.

STRINGS, RANDOM NUMBERS, AND ARRAYS

This chapter revisits and expands upon the core C# programming topics covered in Chapter 3. We look at two core .NET C# base classes: the String class and the Math class. These classes are central to the C# language and are used in even the simplest of applications. The String class contains methods that perform string comparison and manipulation. The Math class contains many useful scientific and trigonometric methods, which we'll use when building the Pong game in Chapter 7. In this chapter you will learn how to:

- Process strings.
- Perform scientific mathematical calculation.
- Generate random numbers.
- Create, loop over, and sort array data structures.
- Design and create a word finder puzzle generator.

PROJECT PREVIEW: GENERATING WORD FINDER PUZZLES

We are going to build a C# Windows Forms application that generates printable word finder puzzles. Word finder puzzles are usually published in magazines and newspapers. Solving a word finder puzzle involves searching for hidden words within a grid (or matrix) of letters. Word finder puzzles are totally addictive. Figure 5-1 displays a word finder puzzle with hidden movie titles. Try to find all five movie titles contained in the puzzle.

The application allows users to create and print word finder puzzles. The user needs to enter the title of the puzzle, as well as the series of words that must be hidden within a matrix of randomly generated characters.

Building this application poses several challenges. First, it must be capable of printing, which hasn't been a requirement in the applications that we've built up to this point. Also, it requires that we write C# code to do the following:

- Generate random characters.
- Store random characters in a two-dimensional (2-D) matrix.
- Split hidden words into characters and embed them within the matrix.
- Display the generated puzzle (i.e., this is actually the 2-D matrix) on a form.
- Print the puzzle on an A4 sheet of paper.

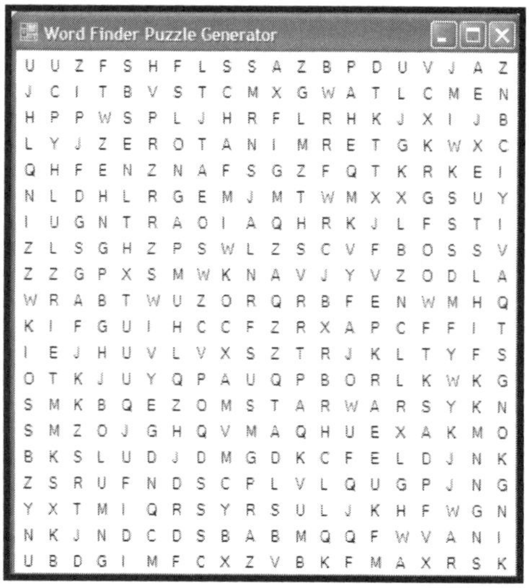

FIGURE 5-1

An example word finder puzzle.

Many of the C# coding concepts required to build this application are covered in this chapter. You will learn how to process strings, generate random numbers, and store data in a 2-D array (matrix). Thus, this is a very rewarding project in terms of the skills that it helps you to develop.

STRINGS

Characters, words, sentences, paragraphs, spaces, punctuation marks, and even numbers can be stored as a string in a variable. Strings are always enclosed within quotations marks and must be declared.

The following are some string variable examples:

```
String word = "Hello";
String sentence = "This is a sentence!";
String letter = "y";
String no = "5";
```

You don't have to declare a variable as a string and assign a value to it at the same time, as illustrated in the next example:

```
String sentence;
sentence = "This is a sentence!";
```

Multiple string variables can be declared simultaneously by separating each variable with a comma:

```
String var1, var2, var3, var4;
```

The String class is a core .NET C# base class. Variables declared as a string are actually objects of the String class. String variables have access to all the methods and properties within the String class. Useful methods within the String class are listed in Table 5-1. In the next few sections, we'll be using these methods to process and manipulate strings.

In the following example, we declare a variable, assign a value to it, and then use the ToUpper() and ToLower() methods to change case:

```
String name = "Aneesha";
String lowercaseName = name.ToLower();
String upperName = name.ToUpper();
```

TABLE 5-1 STRING PROCESSING METHODS WITHIN THE STRING CLASS

Method	Purpose
Compare()	Compares two strings and returns True if they are equal.
Concat()	Joins two strings together.
IndexOf()	Returns the first occurrence of a character or string.
LastIndexOf()	Returns the last occurrence of a character or string.
PadLeft()	Adds spaces to the beginning of a string.
PadRight()	Adds spaces at the end of a string.
Substring()	Extracts a portion of a string.
ToLower()	Converts all characters in a string to lowercase.
ToUpper()	Converts all characters in a string to uppercase.
Trim()	Removes spaces at the beginning and end of a string.
TrimEnd()	Removes spaces at the end of a string.
TrimStart()	Removes spaces at the beginning of a string.

SPECIAL CHARACTERS IN STRINGS

Data that is assigned to a string variable is always enclosed within quotation marks. This raises an interesting question: What if you have to include a quote within a string? The \ is a special escape character that allows you to include quotation marks within the string. The \ escape character must precede the quotation marks embedded within a string.

The following code would cause a syntax error because quotation marks are used in a string without being escaped:

```
String quote = "Celine said "Hello!"";
```

The correct way to include quotation marks is to place a \ in front of each quotation mark:

```
String quote = "Celine said \"Hello!\"";
```

Now, if \ is the escape character, how do you declare a string that includes slashes, such as a file path (for example, c:\temp\files\temp.txt)? The following declaration would also cause a syntax error:

```
String path = "c:\temp\files\";
```

All intentional slashes need to be preceded by the \ escape character. So the declaration of the path should look like the following:

```
String quote = "c:\\temp\\files\\";
```

Table 5-2 lists characters and whitespace symbols that need to be escaped. Even single quotation marks and tabs need to be escaped.

TABLE 5-2 ESCAPE SEQUENCES FOR COMMON WHITESPACE CHARACTERS

Escape Sequence	Special Character
\'	Single quotation mark
\"	Double quotation mark
\\	Backslash
\t	Tab

Placing the @ symbol in front of a string in C# creates a verbatim string. In verbatim strings, there is no need to escape characters. An example of a verbatim string follows:

```
String path = @"c:\temp\files\";
```

Verbatim strings can even span multiple lines:

```
String paragraph = @"This is the first sentence.
This is the second sentence printed on a new line.
This is the third sentence printed on a new line"
```

Finding the Length of a String

It is useful to be able to calculate the number of characters in a string. We'll need to use this functionality in the Word Finder Puzzle Generator because each hidden word must be split into individual characters and embedded within the puzzle's matrix. Sometimes, you'll also need to set a limit on the amount of text that a user can enter into a form element. The Length property of a string variable returns a count of the number of characters stored within the string.

In the following code, we initialize a string variable and then determine the number of characters in the string:

```
String name = "My name is Celine Bakharia";
int noOfChars = name.Length;
```

Converting Numbers to a String

A numeric value can be converted to a string by calling the ToString() method. The ToString() method changes the data type of the value from an integer to a string. Here is an example:

```
int no = 10;
string noAsString = no.ToString();
```

Joining Strings

The process of appending two strings together is known as concatenation. The + operator or the Concat() method can be used to concatenate strings. The following example uses the + operator to construct a sentence containing a user's full name. As you can see, the + operator allows many strings to be appended to each other and stored.

```
String firstname = "Celine";
String surname = "Bakharia";
String sentence = "Welcome " + firstname + " " + surname + ".";
```

The sentence variable will contain the string "Welcome Celine Bakharia."

The Concat() method can only join two strings together:

```
String countTo5 = "12345";
String countTo9 = "6789";
String fullCount = string.Concat(countTo5, countTo9);
```

The fullCount variable will contain the string "123456789".

Changing the Case of a String

We can easily change the case of a string by calling either the ToUpper() method or ToLower() method, depending on the current case of the string. The ToUpper() methods converts all the lowercase characters in a string to uppercase. The ToLower() method does the opposite by converting all uppercase characters stored in the string to lowercase.

In the example that follows, we convert a mixed-case sentence to all uppercase characters and then to all lowercase characters:

```
String mixedCase = "HeLLo! HoW ArE YoU?";
String mixedCase = mixedCase.ToLower();
String mixedCase = mixedCase.ToUpper();
```

String Comparison

Two strings can be compared by using the equal to (==) or not equal to (!=) operators. The String class also contains a Compare() method, which returns a True value if the strings being compared are equal.

In the code that follows, we compare two strings:

```
string answer1 = "madonna";
string answer2 = "MADONNA";
bool checkAnswer = Compare(answer1,answer2);
```

The lowercase and uppercase versions of an answer are compared. The Compare() method in the preceding example will return a False value because it is case sensitive. This means that the strings being compared must have an identical case. We can, however, force the Compare() method to be case insensitive by passing an additional parameter to the method:

```
bool checkAnswer2 = Compare(answer1,answer2,true);
```

This allows us to compare the two answers without using the ToUpper() or ToLower() method to convert both answers to the same case.

Search for and Replace String Data

The Replace() method allows you to search for and replace a sequence of characters within a string. When the Replace() method is called, all occurrences of the search string are replaced. The Replace() method takes two parameters. The first string that is passed to the Replace() method is the substring that you want to replace. The string passed as the second parameter will replace the first parameter when the Replace() method is called.

In the following example, all occurrences of the word car are replaced with the word bicycle:

```
String travel = @"I use a car every day.  The car is a luxury.";
travel = travel.Replace("car", "bicycle");
```

Trim and Pad Strings

The String class even contains methods to remove and add spaces at the beginning or end of a string. The ability to remove extra spaces is particularly useful when you need to process and store data that a user has entered into a form. Sometimes, users accidentally include an extra space after entering the last character of a sentence or word.

The TrimEnd() method removes extra spaces from the end of a string:

```
string Name = "Celine        ";
Name = Name.TrimEnd();
// Name will now be "Celine"
```

The TrimStart() method removes extra spaces from the beginning of a string:

```
string Name = "        Celine ";
Name = Name.TrimStart();
// Name will now be contain "Celine"
```

The Trim() method removes extra spaces from the beginning and end of a string:

```
string Name = "        Celine        ";
Name = Name.Trim();
// Name will now be "Celine"
```

After calling the Trim(), TrimEnd(), and TrimStart() methods, the variable Name will not contain any extra spaces and will be set to "Celine."

We can also add extra spaces to either the beginning or end of a string. The PadLeft() method adds spaces to the beginning of a string, while the PadRight() method adds spaces to the end of the string. An example of using PadLeft() follows:

```
string Sentence = "This is a sentence! ";
Sentence = Sentence.PadLeft(5);
// Sentence will now contain "     This is a sentence!"
```

MATHEMATICS

The Math class is a core .NET C# base class. It contains methods to perform common mathematical calculations and trigonometry. These methods are outlined in Table 5-3. The trigonometry methods within the Math class, such as Sin, Cos, and Tan, will be used extensively when we build the Pong game in subsequent chapters. Something to look forward to!

TABLE 5-3	USEFUL METHODS IN THE MATH CLASS
Method	**Purpose**
Sin	Returns the sine of an angle.
Cos	Returns the cosine of an angle.
Tan	Returns the trigonometric tangent of an angle.
ASin	Returns the arc sine of an angle.
ACos	Returns the arc cosine of an angle.
ATan	Returns the arc tangent of an angle.
ATan2	Converts rectangular coordinates to polar coordinates.
Sqrt	Returns the square root of a number.
Pow	Returns the result after raising a number to a specified power.
Exp	Result of e raised to a specified power.
Log	Returns Natural logarithm of a number.
Abs	Returns Absolute value of a number.
Min	Returns the smaller of two numbers.
Max	Returns the greater of two numbers.
Sign	Returns a sign that indicates whether a number is positive or negative.

In the following example, we calculate the radius of a circle with an area of 16m squared. The Math.Sqrt() method is used to calculate the square root. The constant Math/PI is also used in this example.

```
float radius = Math.Sqrt(16/Math.PI);
```

GENERATING RANDOM NUMBERS

Random numbers are easily generated in C#. The Random class contains a method called Next(), which can generate a random number between 0 and a maximum number that is specified by you. The upper limit of the randomly generated number is passed to the Next() method. It makes sense to define an upper boundary because a purely random number would be useless. In most cases, you'll need to randomly select an item from a set. Examples include displaying random images and quotes.

Let's use the Random class to generate a number between 0 and 10. We'll need to create a Random object, call the Next() method, and pass 10 to it:

```
Random randomObj = new Random();
int  randomNo = randomObj.Next(10);
```

ARRAYS

So far, we have needed to store only a single value in a variable. This has applied to both strings and integers. Suppose we need to store and process the names of all students enrolled in a programming course. We could declare a new variable to store each name. To keep track of our name variables, we could call all of them StudentName and append an incremental number to each to differentiate them. This is illustrated in the next example:

```
String StudentName1 = "Aneesha";
String StudentName2 = "Celine";
String StudentName3 = "Zaeem";
String StudentName4 = "Tess";
```

This does not provide a solution to the problem. We can't write code to iterate over the list and batch-process data. This is where the Array data structure comes in handy. An array is able to store several values of the same type without requiring you to declare a separate name for each variable. Here is our student names example implemented as an array of strings:

```
string[] StudentNames = new string[3];
```

This creates an array that is able to store four values, because the elements are counted from 0. We can now assign the values to the array elements. Square braces are used to reference the elements within the array.

```
StudentNames[0] = "Aneesha";
StudentNames[1] = "Celine";
StudentNames[2] = "Zaeem";
StudentNames[3] = "Tess";
```

Now that we have the names stored in an array, we can use a `for` loop to iterate over the array and do some data processing, as in the following example. The Length property of the array returns the number of elements stored in the array.

```
for (int i = 0; i< StudentNames.Length; i++)
{
        Console.WriteLine(StudentNames [i]);
}
```

We can also use a `foreach` loop to iterate over the array, as follows. The advantage of using a `foreach` loop is that we don't need to explicitly define the length of the array. The `foreach` loop simply iterates over all elements in the array.

```
foreach (int i in StudentNames)
{
        Console.Writeln(i.ToString());
}
```

This is how an array is defined:

```
dataType[] variableName;
```

The data type of an array could be an int, char, or a string. Square braces are placed immediately after the data type.

Arrays must be initialized before a value can be assigned to individual elements. The following code will cause a syntax error because the 10th element in the TestScores array is not initialized before a value is assigned:

```
int[] TestScores;
TestScores[9] = 4;
```

We fix this problem by using the keyword new and initializing the 10 elements within the array:

```
int[] TestScores = new int [9];
We could initialize and assign values at the same time:
int[] TestScores = {1,2,3,4,5};
```

In the next example, we create an integer array to store 10 elements and use a foreach loop to print the contents to the console:

```
int[] TestScores = new int[10];
TestScores[0] = 5;
TestScores[1] = 3;
TestScores[2] = 2;
TestScores[3] = 10;
TestScores[4] = 6;
TestScores[5] = 9;
TestScores[6] = 2;
TestScores[7] = 0;
TestScores[8] = 7;
TestScores[9] = 1;
foreach (int i in TestScores)
{
        Console.Writeln(i.ToString());
}
```

Sorting an Array

The Sort() method arranges the elements in an array in either ascending or alphabetical order:

```
String[] names = {"Aneesha", "Zaeem", "Celine", "Tess"};
//Sorting the contents of an array in alphabetical order
Array.Sort(names);
```

We could also reverse the contents of an array by using the Reverse() method:

```
Array.Reverse(names);
```

Remember that the `foreach` loop provides a simple way to print out or process all elements in an array:

```
foreach (string name in names)
{
        Console.Writeline(name);
}
```

Multidimensional Arrays

The ability to store characters in a 2-D array is crucial to the implementation of the Word Finder Puzzle Generator. This forms the essence of the matrix that will contain hidden words. The WordFinderMatrix is a two-dimensional array with five columns and five rows. Table 5-4 displays the WordFinderMatrix populated with random letters of the alphabet.

TABLE 5-4 THE WORDFINDERMATRIX BUILT USING A 2-D CHARACTER ARRAY					
	0	1	2	3	4
0	d	r	h	j	q
1	h	k	o	r	m
2	c	v	n	h	b
3	z	r	t	n	c
4	q	r	g	y	u

This is how a two-dimensional array is declared and initialized:

```
char[,] WordfinderMatrix = new char[4,4];
```

We can reference individual elements by their index. The following code sets the element in row 1 and column 1 to the letter 'C':

```
WordfinderMatrix [1, 1]  =  'c';
```

We will have to use two for loops to populate the matrix. The first for loop will use a counter variable called i to loop through the five rows of a matrix. The second loop will be placed within the first loop and use the counter variable j to loop through the five columns in the matrix. Placing a loop within another loop is known as a nested loop. The following code fills all of the elements within the matrix with the letter 'A':

```
for (int i = 0; i < 4; i++)
        for (int j = 0; j < 4; j++)
        {
                        WordfinderMatrix [i, j] = 'A';
        }
}
```

We can populate the matrix with random characters by generating a random number between 1 and 26, adding 65 to it, and then casting the number to the char data type, as shown in the following example. We add 65 to the random number to convert it to an upper-case ASCII character.

```
Random randomNo = new Random();
for (int i = 0; i < 4; i++)
        for (int j = 0; j < 4; j++)
        {
                        wordfinderMatrix [i, j] = (char)( randomNo.Next(26) + 65);
        }
}
```

BACK TO THE WORD FINDER PUZZLE GENERATOR

We return to complete our ambitious project, the Word Finder Puzzle Generator. We know how to create a 2-D matrix and populate it with random characters. Our task now is to place words within the matrix and then populate the remaining elements with random characters.

Designing the Interface

We do not need to do a lot of interface design, as Figure 5-2 demonstrates. All we need is a form that we can print the character matrix on. The size of the form does not matter because we will change it programmatically.

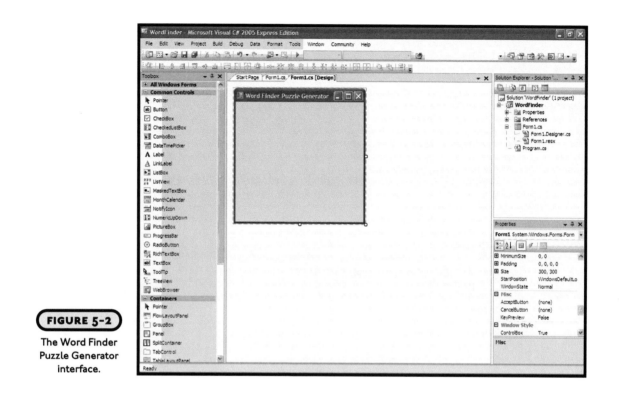

FIGURE 5-2

The Word Finder
Puzzle Generator
interface.

Creating the WordFinder form:

1. Create a new Windows Forms application called WordFinder.

2. Set the Text property of the form to Word Finder Puzzle Generator. This will change
   the title of the form.

Adding the C# Code

We are now going to write the C# code for the most challenging application we have
encountered thus far in the book. All of the code needs to be placed within the Form1.cs file
in the Form1 class. To keep the code simple and manageable, we separate the code into logical sections and place each into a method. We are going to build a 20 by 20 character matrix.
We need to declare and initialize the following variables within the Form1 class:

```
namespace WordFinder
using System;
using System.Collections.Generic;
using System.ComponentModel;
using System.Data;
```

```
using System.Drawing;
using System.Text;
using System.Windows.Forms;

namespace WordFinder
{
    public partial class Form1 : Form
    {
        string[] words = new string[5] { "Alien", "Terminator", "StarWars",
"KingKong", "Speed" };
        const int noRows = 20;
        const int noCols = 20;
        char[,] WordFinderMatrix = new char[noRows, noCols];
        int WordFinderMatrixSpacing = 20;
        int WordFinderMatrixPadding = 5;
        Graphics g;
        public Form1()
        {
        }
        void InitializeWordFinderMatrix()
        {
        }
        private void InsertWords()
        {
        }
        private bool InsertWord(String word, int row, int col, int xDirection,
int yDirection)
        {
        }
        private void FillWordFinder()
        {
        }
        private void PaintWordFinder(object
sender,System.Windows.Forms.PaintEventArgs e)
        {
        }
    }
}
```

The WordFinderMatrixSpacing and WordFinderMatrixPadding variables will be used to lay out the letters in the matrix when they are printed onto the form. The matrix variable is a 2-D array that has 20 columns and 20 rows. The words array stores the hidden words.

The Form1() method needs to set the bounds of the form. This calculation is based upon the number of columns and rows, as well as the WordFinderMatrixSpacing and WordFinderMatrixPadding variables. The InitializeWordFinderMatrix() method is called. This method sets each element in the matrix to a blank character. The InsertWords() method inserts the hidden words into the matrix. The FillWordFinder() method replaces all the blank characters with a random character.

```
public Form1()
        {
                int FormWidth = noRows * WordFinderMatrixSpacing +
WordFinderMatrixPadding + 5;
                int FormHeight = (noCols + 1) * WordFinderMatrixSpacing +
WordFinderMatrixPadding + 10;

                InitializeComponent();
                this.Paint += new PaintEventHandler(PaintWordFinder);
                this.SetBounds(0, 0, FormWidth, FormHeight);
                InitializeWordFinderMatrix();
                InsertWords();
                FillWordFinder();
        }
```

InitializeWordFinderMatrix() simply uses two loops to fill the 2-D array with a space:

```
        void InitializeWordFinderMatrix()
        {
        int i;
        int j;
        // Make each character position in the WordFinderMatrix blank
        for (i = 0; i < noRows; i++)
        {
                for (j = 0; j < noCols; j++)
                {
                        WordFinderMatrix[i, j] = ' ';
                }
        }
        }
```

InsertWords() uses a foreach loop to iterate over the words that must be hidden within the matrix. Each word is trimmed to remove extra spaces at the beginning or end of the word. Each word is also converted to uppercase before it is placed by the InsertWords() method. A random row and column value is generated and passed to the InsertWords() method, which will add the word to the matrix.

```
private void InsertWords()
            {
                Random RandonNo = new Random();

                foreach (String word in words)
                {
                    bool WordInserted = false;

                    String currentWord = word.Trim();
                    currentWord = currentWord.ToUpper();

                    while (WordInserted == false)
                    {
                        int randomXDirection = 0;
                        int randomYDirection = 0;

                        int randomRow = RandonNo.Next(noRows);
                        int randomCol = RandonNo.Next(noCols);

                        while ((randomXDirection == 0) && (randomYDirection
== 0))
                        {
                            randomXDirection = RandonNo.Next(3) - 1;
                            randomYDirection = RandonNo.Next(3) - 1;
                        }

                    WordInserted = InsertWord(currentWord, randomRow,
randomCol, randomXDirection, randomYDirection);
                    }
                }
            }
```

The InsertWord() method first checks if there is space in the current row to fit all charac-ters. If not, it returns False, and the InsertWord() method will need to generate a random row and column again. InsertWord() also checks that all the none space characters will be overwritten. If these two tests pass, each letter of the hidden word is assigned to the appro-priate array elements.

```csharp
private bool InsertWord(String word, int row, int col, int xDirection,
int yDirection)
        {
                int wordLength = word.Length;
                int i;

                // check if no of letters in word will be able
                // to be inserted given the position (row and column) and
                // the no of letter spaces available in the matrix
                if (xDirection > 0)
                {
                        if (row + wordLength > noRows)
                        {
                                return false;
                        }
                }
                if (yDirection > 0)
                {
                        if (col + wordLength > noCols)
                        {
                                return false;
                        }
                }
                if (xDirection < 0)
                {
                        if (row - wordLength < 0)
                        {
                                return false;
                        }
                }
                if (yDirection < 0)
```

```
            {
                if (col - wordLength < 0)
                {
                        return false;
                }
            }

            // check if another word is already inserted at
            // col and row position
            for (i = 0; i < wordLength; i++)
            {
                    int matrixXPos = row + (xDirection * i);
                    int matrixYPos = col + (yDirection * i);
                    if (WordFinderMatrix[matrixXPos, matrixYPos] != ' ')
                    {
                            return false;
                    }
            }

            // OK to insert word into WordFinderMatrix
            for (i = 0; i < word.Length; i++)
            {
                    int matrixXPos = row + (xDirection * i);
                    int matrixYPos = col + (yDirection * i);
                    WordFinderMatrix[matrixXPos, matrixYPos] = word[i];
            }

            return true;
    }
```

The FillWordFinder() method replaces all space characters with a random letter of the alphabet:

```
        private void FillWordFinder()
        {
                int i;
                int j;
                Random randomNo = new Random();
```

```
            for (i = 0; i < noRows; i++)
            {
                    for (j = 0; j < noCols; j++)
                    {
                            // If a position within the WordFinderMatrix is
```
blank
```
                            // fill it with a random uppercase character
                            if (WordFinderMatrix[i, j] == ' ')
                            {
                                    WordFinderMatrix[i, j] =
```
(char)(randomNo.Next(26) + 65);
```
                            }
                    }
            }
        }
```

We need to implement a PaintWordFinder() method so that we can get the graphics context of the form and print the contents of the matrix. We use the FillRectangle() method to draw a white background on the form. We use the DrawString() method to print the letters onto the form.

```
            private void PaintWordFinder(object
sender,System.Windows.Forms.PaintEventArgs e)
            {
                    int i;
                    int j;
                    g = e.Graphics;
                    // Make the Background White
                    g.FillRectangle(Brushes.White, ClientRectangle);
                    // Draw each character in the WordFinderMatrix
                    for (i = 0; i < noRows; i++)
                    {
                            for (j = 0; j < noCols; j++)
                            {
                                    // Calculate the x and y position of each character
                                    int charXPos = i * WordFinderMatrixSpacing +
WordFinderMatrixPadding;
```

```
                                int charYPos = j * WordFinderMatrixSpacing +
WordFinderMatrixPadding;
                                g.DrawString(WordFinderMatrix[i, j].ToString(),
this.Font, Brushes.Black, charXPos, charYPos);
                        }
                }
        }
```

The final code should look like this:

```csharp
using System;
using System.Collections.Generic;
using System.ComponentModel;
using System.Data;
using System.Drawing;
using System.Text;
using System.Windows.Forms;

namespace WordFinder
{
    public partial class Form1 : Form
    {

        string[] words = new string[5] { "Alien", "Terminator", "StarWars",
"KingKong", "Speed" };

        const int noRows = 20;
        const int noCols = 20;

        char[,] WordFinderMatrix = new char[noRows, noCols];

        int WordFinderMatrixSpacing = 20;
        int WordFinderMatrixPadding = 5;

        Graphics g;

        public Form1()
        {
```

```
            int FormWidth = noRows * WordFinderMatrixSpacing +
WordFinderMatrixPadding + 5;
            int FormHeight = (noCols + 1) * WordFinderMatrixSpacing +
WordFinderMatrixPadding + 10;

        InitializeComponent();
        this.Paint += new PaintEventHandler(PaintWordFinder);
        this.SetBounds(0, 0, FormWidth, FormHeight);
        InitializeWordFinderMatrix();
        InsertWords();
        FillWordFinder();
    }

    void InitializeWordFinderMatrix()
    {
        int i;
        int j;

        // Make each character position in the WordFinderMatrix blank
        for (i = 0; i < noRows; i++)
        {
            for (j = 0; j < noCols; j++)
            {
                WordFinderMatrix[i, j] = ' ';
            }
        }
    }

    private void InsertWords()
    {
        Random RandonNo = new Random();

        foreach (String word in words)
        {
            bool WordInserted = false;
```

```csharp
                String currentWord = word.Trim();
                currentWord = currentWord.ToUpper();

                while (WordInserted == false)
                {
                        int randomXDirection = 0;
                        int randomYDirection = 0;

                        int randomRow = RandonNo.Next(noRows);
                        int randomCol = RandonNo.Next(noCols);

                        while ((randomXDirection == 0) && (randomYDirection
== 0))

                        {
                                randomXDirection = RandonNo.Next(3) - 1;
                                randomYDirection = RandonNo.Next(3) - 1;
                        }

                        WordInserted = InsertWord(currentWord, randomRow,
randomCol, randomXDirection, randomYDirection);
                }
        }
    }

        private bool InsertWord(String word, int row, int col, int xDirection,
int yDirection)
        {
                int wordLength = word.Length;
                int i;

                // check if no of letters in word will be able
                // to be inserted given the position (row and column) and
                // the no of letter spaces available in the matrix
                if (xDirection > 0)
                {
                        if (row + wordLength > noRows)
```

```
    {
        return false;
    }
}
if (yDirection > 0)
{
    if (col + wordLength > noCols)
    {
        return false;
    }
}
if (xDirection < 0)
{
    if (row - wordLength < 0)
    {
        return false;
    }
}
if (yDirection < 0)
{
    if (col - wordLength < 0)
    {
        return false;
    }
}

// check if another word is already inserted at
// col and row position
for (i = 0; i < wordLength; i++)
{
    int matrixXPos = row + (xDirection * i);
    int matrixYPos = col + (yDirection * i);
    if (WordFinderMatrix[matrixXPos, matrixYPos] != ' ')
    {
        return false;
    }
```

```csharp
                }

                // OK to insert word into WordFinderMatrix
                for (i = 0; i < word.Length; i++)
                {
                        int matrixXPos = row + (xDirection * i);
                        int matrixYPos = col + (yDirection * i);
                        WordFinderMatrix[matrixXPos, matrixYPos] = word[i];
                }

                return true;
        }

        private void FillWordFinder()
        {
                int i;
                int j;
                Random randomNo = new Random();
                for (i = 0; i < noRows; i++)
                {
                        for (j = 0; j < noCols; j++)
                        {
                                // If a position within the WordFinderMatrix is
blank
                                // fill it with a random uppercase character
                                if (WordFinderMatrix[i, j] == ' ')
                                {
                                        WordFinderMatrix[i, j] =
(char)(randomNo.Next(26) + 65);
                                }
                        }
                }
        }

        private void PaintWordFinder(object
```

```
sender,System.Windows.Forms.PaintEventArgs e)
        {
                int i;
                int j;
                g = e.Graphics;
                // Make the Background White
                g.FillRectangle(Brushes.White, ClientRectangle);
                // Draw each character in the WordFinderMatrix
                for (i = 0; i < noRows; i++)
                {
                        for (j = 0; j < noCols; j++)
                        {
                                // Calculate the x and y position of each character
                                int charXPos = i * WordFinderMatrixSpacing +
WordFinderMatrixPadding;

                                int charYPos = j * WordFinderMatrixSpacing +
WordFinderMatrixPadding;

                                g.DrawString(WordFinderMatrix[i, j].ToString(),
this.Font, Brushes.Black, charXPos, charYPos);
                        }
                }
        }
}
```

Testing the Application

This is not an easy application to test. One way would be to visually find all of the hidden words each time a puzzle is generated. This might be fun if you really like solving puzzles. The smart way, however, would be to change the color of the characters that make up the hidden words. We would do this with the following one line of code, which prints the answers in bold and in the color red:

```
g.DrawString(WordFinderMatrix[i, j].ToString(), this.Font, Brushes.Red, charXPos,
charYPos);
```

SUMMARY

You've learned a lot about using strings, math, random numbers, and arrays in C#. You've also designed and built a very impressive and challenging Word Finder Puzzle Generator. You will need to apply the string processing techniques introduced in this chapter in just about all C# programs that you will build. You've also started to design, program, and problem solve algorithms, such as the algorithm used to populate the WordFinderMatrix with random characters and insert hidden words within the matrix. Algorithms are a very important element of programming, and we'll certainly have to implement many more in future chapters.

CHALLENGES

1. Write a program to calculate the area of a circle. The radius of the circle is 2 cm.

2. Create an application that displays random images.

3. Calculate and display the number of days until Christmas.

4. Enhance the Word Finder Puzzle Generator so that it is able to print solutions to the generated puzzles as well.

DRAWING GRAPHICS AND BUILDING GAMES

The ability to dynamically draw and update graphics is essential when building games. .NET has excellent graphics creation and manipulation features that are easily accessible through the C# language. Animation, controlling objects with a mouse, and collision detection are core game programming techniques. Once you have mastered these concepts, the only limit will be your imagination. This is going to be a fun chapter. In this chapter you will learn how to:

- Draw lines, ellipses, rectangles, and text on a form.
- Animate objects.
- Detect collisions between objects.
- Respond to mouse movement.
- Design and build the Pong Game.

PROJECT PREVIEW: THE PONG GAME

The Pong Game is a very ambitious project. Of the games that you have designed, programmed, and tested thus far in the book, the Pong Game is certainly the most sophisticated. This does not mean that building this game is going to be difficult. The game utilizes simple concepts, all of which are covered in this chapter.

We are going to build a single-player Pong Game. The purpose is to stop a ball from bouncing off the wall that you are defending. There are four walls, and the ball is allowed to bounce off the other three walls. The player hits the ball with a paddle that is controlled (moved) with the mouse. The interface is shown in Figure 6-1.

To complete this game, you need to be able to program the following features, as described in the following sections:

- Draw a ball (circle).
- Animate a ball.
- Check if the ball has collided with a wall.
- Reflect a ball off a wall if it has collided with a wall.
- Move a paddle with the mouse.
- Check if the ball has collided with the paddle (player has hit the ball).
- Reflect a ball off the paddle if it has collided with a paddle.

FIGURE 6-1

The Pong Game.

THE GRAPHICS CLASS

Conceptually, the tools that you use in a C# program to draw shapes on a form are similar to the tools that you use to draw shapes on a piece of paper: a set of colored pens or paint brushes, and methods, similar to stencils, to draw shapes. Drawing with C# and the .NET Framework is very similar. You have pens and brushes, methods to draw shapes, and a drawing surface. You still need to bring the creative flair.

We use the Graphics class to create a canvas or drawing surface. Before we can use the Graphics class, however, we must reference the System.Drawing and System.Drawing.Drawing2D namespaces. Once we have a graphics surface, we can then draw arcs, circles, and rectangles, by using the methods of the Graphics class, which are listed and described in Table 6-1. The Paint event of a form is used to get a reference to the Graphics object.

TABLE 6-1   DRAWING SHAPES WITH THE GRAPHICS CLASS'S METHODS

Method	Purpose
DrawArc()	Draws an arc.
DrawBézier()	Draws a Bézier curve.
DrawBéziers()	Draws a specified number of Bézier curves.
DrawCurve()	Draws a curve as specified by points in an array.
DrawEllipse()	Draws an ellipse.
DrawImage()	Draws an image.
DrawLine()	Draws a line.
DrawPath()	Draws lines and curves.
DrawPie()	Draws a pie section.
DrawPolygon()	Draws a polygon.
DrawRectangle()	Draws a rectangle.
DrawString()	Draws text in a specified font.
FillEllipse()	Draws a filled ellipse.
FillPath()	Fills the interior of a path.
FillPie()	Fills a pie section.
FillPolygon()	Fills a polygon.
FillRectangle()	Fills a rectangle.

The following code shows how to get a reference to the Graphics object on Form1:

```
Private void Form1_Paint( object sender, PaintEventArgs e)
{
        Graphics g = e.Graphics;
}
```

Let's build a simple program to draw some text and a line on a form:

1. Create a new Windows Forms application called SimpleGraphics.

2. Set the Width of the Form to 400 and the Height to 300.

3. Press F7 to display the code for Form1.

4. Add a `PaintEventHandler` to the `Form1()` constructor. This is what the `Form1()` constructor method will contain:

   ```
   public Form1()
   {
           InitializeComponent();
           this.Paint += new PaintEventHandler(Form1_paint);
   }
   ```

5. Create a `Form1_paint()` method within the `Form1` class:

   ```
   private void Form1_paint( object sender, PaintEventArgs e)
   {

   }
   ```

6. Add the C# code to draw a string and a line on the form:

   ```
   // Get Graphics Object
   Graphics g = e.Graphics;
   // Create a Font
   Font font = new Font("Verdana", 30);
   // Create a Brush
   SolidBrush brush = new SolidBrush(Color.Blue);
   // Draw the String
   g.DrawString("C# Says Hello!", font, brush, 40, 40);
   // Create a Pen
   Pen pen = new Pen(Color.Red, 4);
   ```

```
// Draw the Line
g.DrawLine(pen, 60, 200, 300, 200);
// Dispose all objects
font.Dispose();
brush.Dispose();
pen.Dispose();
```

Figure 6-2 shows the graphics drawn onto a form. To draw text on the form, we used the DrawString() method but also needed Font and Brush objects. We also used the DrawLine() method to draw a line and needed a Pen object. Table 6-2 details the important objects within the Graphics class. The coordinates for drawing objects are specified from the top-left corner of the form.

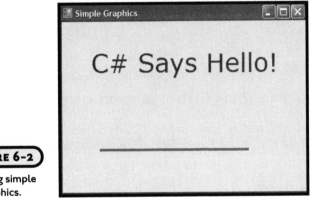

Drawing simple graphics.

TABLE 6-2	OBJECTS OF THE GRAPHICS CLASS
Object	**Description**
Pen	Used to draw lines.
Brush	Used to fill shapes with patterns, images, or flat colors.
Font	Used to set a font for text drawn on the canvas.
Color	Used to represent an Alpha Red Green Blue (ARGB) color.

The Pen Class

The Pen object is modeled off a real pen. It has a color and a width. The Pen object is created by calling a constructor. Remember that constructors initialize an object. The Pen object is used to draw the outline of an object. We will use a Brush object if we want to fill an object.

This code creates a Pen object that is blue in color:

```
Pen myPen = new Pen(Color.Blue);
Here we create a Pen object that is blue in color and has a width of 100:
Pen myPen = new Pen(Color.Blue, 100);
```

The Font Class

The Font object specifies a font, its size, and its style. Here is the syntax for calling the Font() constructor:

```
public Font (fontname , FontStyle);
or
public Font (fontname , float)
```

FontStyle is an enumeration. FontStyle could be Bold, Italic, Regular, Strikeout, or Underline.

This example creates a Font object that uses the Times New Roman font and is 26 points in size:

```
Font font = new Font ("Times New Roman", 26);
```

The method DrawString() takes the five arguments and prints text to the graphics canvas. The next code snippet prints "Hello C#" in pink to the screen with a 30-point Times New Roman font. The x coordinate is 80 pixels and the y coordinate is 40 pixels.

```
Graphics g = e.Graphics;
g.DrawString( "Hello C#",
            new Font( " Times New Roman ",30 ),
            new SolidBrush( Color.Pink ),
            80,
            80);
```

The Brush Class

The Brush class can fill shapes with a solid color, pattern, or image. Remember that you must use the Pen object if you only want to create an outline of the shape. There are four types of Brush objects: SolidBrush, HatchBrush, GradientBrush, and TextureBrush.

The SolidBrush object is the default brush. It simply fills a shape with a solid color. The following is the code to create a rectangle filled with a red color using the SolidBrush object, the result of which is shown in Figure 6-3:

```
Graphics g = e.Graphics;
Graphics g = e.Graphics;
SolidBrush solidbrush = new SolidBrush( Color.Red );
g.FillRectangle(solidbrush, 50, 50, 200, 200 );
```

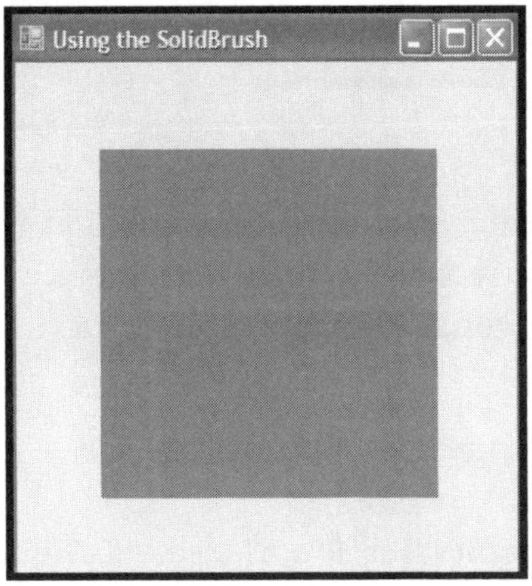

FIGURE 6-3

Using the
SolidBrush
object.

The HatchBrush object fills an object with a hatch pattern. HatchStyle specifies the type of hatch pattern and can be Cross, DiagonalCross, ForwardDiagonal, Horizontal, Vertical, or Solid. In the following code excerpt, we fill a rectangle with a red and blue cross pattern, as shown in Figure 6-4:

```
Graphics g = e.Graphics;
HatchStyle hatchstyle = HatchStyle.Cross;
HatchBrush hatchbrush = new HatchBrush( hatchstyle, Color.Blue, Color.Red );
g.FillRectangle( hatchbrush, 50, 50, 200, 200 );
```

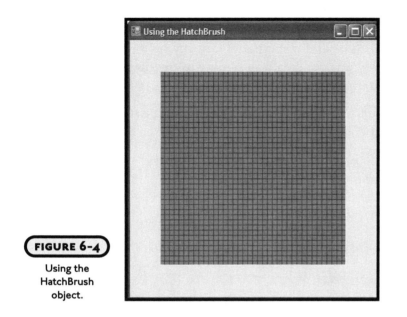

FIGURE 6-4

Using the
HatchBrush
object.

The GradientBrush object fills a shape with a gradient color transition from one color to another. LinearGradientMode enumeration sets the gradient direction, which can be ForwardDiagonal (see Figure 6-5), BackwardDiagonal, Horizontal, or Vertical.

```
    Graphics g = e.Graphics;
    LinearGradientMode lgm = LinearGradientMode.ForwardDiagonal;
    Rectangle rect = new Rectangle(3, 3, 10, 10);
    LinearGradientBrush lgb = new LinearGradientBrush( rect, Color.Blue,
Color.Red, lgm );
    g.FillRectangle( lgb, 50, 50, 200, 200 );
```

The TextureBrush object paints an image within the bounds of a shape. The following example draws an ellipse with a background image, as shown in Figure 6-6:

```
    Graphics g = e.Graphics;
    Image bgimage = new Bitmap( "flowers.gif" );
    Brush   bgbrush = new TextureBrush( bgimage );
    g.FillEllipse( bgbrush, 50, 50, 500, 300 );
```

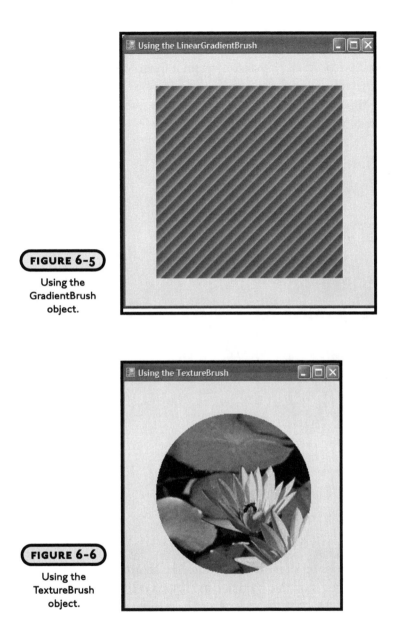

FIGURE 6-5

Using the
GradientBrush
object.

FIGURE 6-6

Using the
TextureBrush
object.

WORKING WITH IMAGES

In Chapter 1, we used a PictureBox control to display an image on a form. We are now going to use the DrawImage() method to dynamically print an image on a form (see Figure 6-7). The DrawImage() method is much more flexible than the PictureBox control. We first need to create a Bitmap object and pass the DrawImage() method to it:

```
Graphics g = e.Graphics;
      Image img = new Bitmap( "flowers.gif" );
      g.DrawImage( img, 10, 10, 100, 100 );
```

Drawing an image.

DRAWING LINES

The DrawLine() method, as its name suggests, draws a line connecting two points, as shown in Figure 6-8. The points are specified by x and y coordinate pairs. The coordinate pairs could be of either type integer or type float. The starting point of the line is (x1, y1) and the ending point is (x2, y2). The syntax is as follows:

```
public void DrawLine( Pen, int x1, int y1, int x2, int y2 );
```

or

```
public void DrawLine( Pen, float x1, float y1, float x2, float y2 );
```

We could also specify the coordinates by using a Point object. The syntax would then be as follows:

```
public void DrawLine( Pen, Point pt1, Point pt2 );
```

or

```
public void DrawLine( Pen, PointF pt1, PointF pt2 );
```

Here is an example of using the DrawLine() method with Point objects:

```
Graphics g = e.Graphics;
Pen myPen = new Pen(Color.Blue,100);
g.DrawLine(myPen, new Point(10, 10), new Point(200, 200));
```

FIGURE 6-8

Drawing a line.

DRAWING RECTANGLES

The DrawRectangle() method uses a Pen object to draw an unfilled rectangle on the drawing canvas, which in our case is the background of a form:

```
public void DrawRectangle( Pen pen, int x, int y, int width, int height );
```

or

```
public void DrawRectangle( Pen pen, float x, float y, float width, float height );
```

The following parameters are passed to the DrawRectangle() method:

- The Pen object (draws the outline of the rectangle)
- The x coordinate
- The y coordinate
- The width of the rectangle
- The height of the rectangle

Here we draw a rectangle with a blue outline that has a width of five pixels:

```
Graphics g = e.Graphics;
Pen pen = new Pen( Color.Blue, 5 );
g.DrawRectangle(pen, 10, 10, 200, 200 );
```

We can also draw a filled rectangle by using the FillRectangle() method. The type of fill is specified with a Brush object, as follows:

```
Graphics g = e.Graphics;
SolidBrush blueBrush = new SolidBrush(Color.Blue);
g.FillRectangle( blueBrush, 20, 20, 100, 100);
```

Figure 6-9 show the output of both the DrawRectangle() and the FillRectangle() methods.

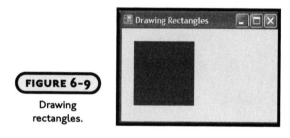

FIGURE 6-9

Drawing
rectangles.

DRAWING ELLIPSES

The DrawEllipse() method can also be used to draw circles. The DrawEllipse() method takes five parameters. These methods draw an ellipse specified by a coordinate pair, a width, and a height. The syntax for the DrawEllipse() method is as follows:

```
public void DrawEllipse( Pen pen, int x, int y, int width, int height );
```

or

```
public void DrawEllipse( Pen pen, float x, float y, float width, float height );
```

We will create a simple example to draw an ellipse on the form:

```
Graphics g = e.Graphics;
Pen pen = new Pen( Color.Blue, 2 );
g.DrawEllipse( pen, 10, 10, 200, 300 );
```

The FillEllipse() method draws a filled ellipse. Here we draw an ellipse with a solid color fill:

```
Graphics g = e.Graphics;
Graphics g = e.Graphics;
SolidBrush brush = new SolidBrush(Color.Blue);
g.FillEllipse( brush, 10, 10, 200, 300 );
```

Figure 6-10 show the output of both the DrawEllipse() and FillEllipse() methods.

FIGURE 6-10

Drawing ellipses.

ANIMATION AND COLLISION DETECTION

The Pong Game relies on our ability to draw a ball and bounce it off the bounding walls of a form (see Figure 6-11). This means that we need to be able to move a ball in one direction until it collides with a wall, and then change the direction of the ball so that the ball appears to bounce off the wall.

The following are some variables that we need to declare:

```
int x = 0; // initial x position of the ball
int y = 0; // initial y position of the ball
int dx = 8; // position increment for the ball on the x axis
int dy = 5; // position increment for the ball on the y axis
Graphics g; // the graphics context
```

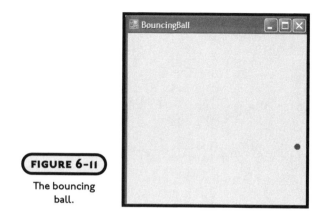

The first thing we need to accomplish with our C# code is to draw a ball on the background of the form. We can use the `FillEllipse()` method to do this within our form's `PaintEventHandler`:

```
public Form1()
{
        InitializeComponent();
        this.Paint += new PaintEventHandler(Form1_paint);
}

private void Form1_ paint(Object sender, PaintEventArgs e)
{
        g = e.Graphics;
        SolidBrush brush = new SolidBrush(Color.Blue);
        g.FillEllipse(brush, x, y, 5, 5);
}
```

We then need to move the ball at regular intervals. We can use the Timer control to trigger a `moveBall()` method every few milliseconds. Don't forget to set the Enabled property of the Timer to true. Here the `timer1_Tick()` method calls the `moveBall()` method periodically:

```
private void timer1_Tick(object sender, EventArgs e)
{
        moveBall();
}
private void moveBall()
{
```

```
        x = x + dx;
        y = y + dy;
        Invalidate();
    }
```

Calling the `Invalidate()` method causes a form to run its `PaintEventHandler`, which in this case is the `Form1_paint()` method. This method draws the ball at its new x and y coordinates. We still have a problem because our ball will move past the bounding walls of the form.

Our next step is to detect the collision of the ball with a wall and then change the direction of the ball. This is easily achieved by comparing the ball's x and y coordinates with the coordinates of the bounding walls. This code needs to be placed within the `moveBall()` method.

```
private void moveBall()
{
    if ((x + dx < 0) || (x + dx > 300)) dx = -dx;
    if ((y + dy < 0) || (y + dy > 255)) dy = -dy;
    x = x + dx;
    y = y + dy;
    Invalidate();
}
```

MOVING AN OBJECT WITH A MOUSE

In the Pong Game, the player needs to be able to move a paddle to stop the ball from bouncing off the bottom (floor) of a form (see Figure 6-12). The easiest way to do this is to get the paddle to follow the mouse.

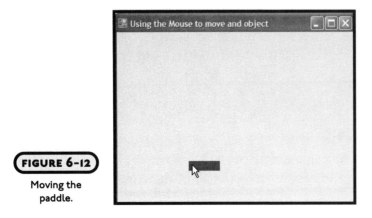

FIGURE 6-12

Moving the paddle.

The following are the variables that we need to declare:

```
int x; // the x coordinate of the paddle
int y; // the y coordinate of the paddle
Graphics g; // the graphics context
```

The forms constructor method needs to add MouseMove and PaintEventHandler:

```
public Form1()
{
    InitializeComponent();
    this.MouseMove += new MouseEventHandler(movePaddle);
    this.Paint += new PaintEventHandler(paint1);
}
```

The paint event handler simply draws the paddle at the new x and y coordinates. The FillRectangle() method is used to draw the paddle:

```
private void paint1(Object sender, PaintEventArgs e)
{
    g = e.Graphics;
    SolidBrush blueBrush = new SolidBrush(Color.Blue);
    g.FillRectangle(blueBrush, x-5, y-5, 50, 15);
}
```

The MouseMove event handler needs to set the x and y coordinates of the paddle to the mouse's x and y coordinates. The Invalidate() method is then set to make sure the form is painted again to reflect the movement of the paddle:

```
private void movePaddle(Object sender, MouseEventArgs e)
{
    y = e.Y;
    x = e.X;
    Invalidate();
}
```

BACK TO THE PONG GAME

All of the ingredients are in place. We can animate the ball, bounce the ball off the walls, and move the paddle with a mouse. We need to combine all of these techniques to create our Pong Game.

Designing the Interface

The interface is very simple; we just need a form with a green background, a Timer control, a ball, and a movable paddle. The ball and paddle will be drawn dynamically by C# code.

1. Create a new Windows Forms application called Pong.

2. Set the BackColor property of the form to green.

3. Set the size of the form to 300 × 300.

4. Set the Text property of the form to "The Pong Game."

5. Drag a Timer control onto the form. Set the Enabled property to True.

Programming the C# Code

We need to combine the code from the "Animation and Collision Detection" and "Moving an Object with a Mouse" sections. We also need to detect the collision between the paddle and the ball. Here is the full C# code listing:

```
using System;
using System.Collections.Generic;
using System.ComponentModel;
using System.Data;
using System.Drawing;
using System.Text;
using System.Windows.Forms;

namespace Pong
{
    public partial class Form1 : Form
    {
        int paddle_x = 0;
        int paddle_y = 255;
        int paddle_width = 35;
        int paddle_height = 20;
        Graphics g;
        int x = 0; // initial x position of the ball
        int y = 0; // initial y position of the ball
        int dx = 8; // position increment for the ball on the x axis
```

```csharp
        int dy = 5; // position increment for the ball on the y axis

        public Form1()
        {
            InitializeComponent();
            this.MouseMove += new MouseEventHandler(MovePaddle);
            this.Paint += new PaintEventHandler(paint1);
        }

        private void paint1(Object sender, PaintEventArgs e)
        {
            g = e.Graphics;
            // draw the paddle
            SolidBrush blueBrush = new SolidBrush(Color.Red);
            g.FillRectangle(blueBrush, paddle_x, paddle_y, paddle_width, paddle_height);

            // draw the ball
            SolidBrush brush = new SolidBrush(Color.Blue);
            g.FillEllipse(brush, x, y, 10, 10);
        }

        private void MovePaddle(Object sender, MouseEventArgs e)
        {
            paddle_y = e.Y;
            paddle_x = e.X;
            Invalidate();
        }

        private void timer1_Tick(object sender, EventArgs e)
        {
            MoveBall();
        }

        private void MoveBall()
        {
            int newBall_x = x + dx;
            int newBall_y = y + dy;
```

```
// Bounce the ball if it has collided with a wall
if ((newBall_x < 0) || (newBall_x > 300)) dx = -dx;
if ((newBall_y < 0) || (newBall_y > 255)) dy = -dy;

// Bounce the ball if it has collided with the paddle
if (((newBall_x > paddle_x) && (newBall_x < (paddle_x +
paddle_width)))&&((newBall_y > paddle_y) && (newBall_y < (paddle_y +
paddle_height))))
        {
                if (dx > 0 && dy > 0)
                {
                        dy = -dy;
                }
                if (dx < 0 && dy > 0)
                {
                        dy = -dy;
                }
        }
        x = x + dx;
        y = y + dy;
        Invalidate();
        }
    }
}
```

Testing the Game

The best way to test the Pong Game is to have fun and spend many hours playing it. You need to make sure that the ball bounces off all the walls and that the paddle is always able to hit the ball. While testing the application, think of ways to enhance the game. I'm sure family members are eager to play the game as well.

SUMMARY

This chapter has covered a lot of really cool graphics and game programming concepts. You have learned how to draw and animate shapes, control an element with a mouse, and detect collisions between objects. These concepts, when combined, form the ingredients of a dynamic and addictive game. This is evident by the rich functionality that we were able to program into the Pong Game. I'm sure you'll agree that C# is both a simple and a powerful language. There is much more to learn, though, and Chapter 7 will expand upon the concepts covered in this chapter. In Chapter 7, you'll build an application that uses the mouse to draw shapes on a form.

CHALLENGES

1. Design an application that is able to draw a line graph from the following arrays of x and y values:

```
int[] x = { 400, 100, 200, 700, 900 };
int[] y = { 25, 15, 70, 100, 75 };
```

2. Design an interface for the graphing application that you built in Challenge 1. The interface will allow a user to enter the x and y values that need to be plotted.

3. Write a graphics program that draws a house, a fence, the sun, and some clouds onto the background of a Windows form.

4. Extend the Pong Game to include a virtual opponent. This will allow the user to play against the computer.

DESIGNING ADVANCED WINDOWS FORMS APPLICATIONS

An interface can contain much more than just simple Button and TextBox controls. Many of the applications that you use on a daily basis, such as Microsoft Internet Explorer and Microsoft Word, consist of more advanced controls like the Menu, ToolStrip, Tab, and TreeView controls. Visual C# Express makes adding these controls to an application a breeze. You'll be building professional looking application in no time at all. In this chapter you will learn how to:

- Use the Timer control.
- Use the DateTimePicker control.
- Add tabbed dialog boxes to a form.
- Use the TreeView control.
- Add a menu to a Windows Forms application.
- Add a ToolBar control to an application.
- Design and program a drawing application in C#.

PROJECT PREVIEW: SHARP PAINTING — A DRAWING APPLICATION

We are going to design and program a C# painting application called Sharp Painting (see Figure 7-1). The application will enable users to use a mouse to draw rectangles and circles onscreen. This application implements the graphics concepts that you learned in Chapter 6. We will also be implementing a few of the advanced interface elements covered in this chapter, such as menus and toolbars.

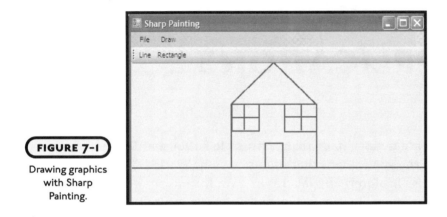

FIGURE 7-1

Drawing graphics with Sharp Painting.

WINDOWS FORMS CONTROLS — A RECAP

Visual C# 2005 Express Edition includes many graphical user interface controls. Although it is not practical to cover all the controls in this book, that does not mean that you won't be able to use these controls, of course. It is important to remember that the processes of adding controls, setting control properties, and writing code to respond to events such as clicking on a control are always the same.

The DateTimePicker control (see Figure 7-2) allows a user to select and specify a date from a calendar. To use this control on a form, simply drag the DateTimePicker control from the Toolbox onto a form.

The DateTimePicker control's properties are shown in Figure 7-2. The two most important properties are the Value, which contains the initial date displayed by the control, and the Format, which sets the date format.

After you have added the DateTimePicker control to the form, press F5 to run the sample application. The current date is displayed with a drop-down arrow next to it. Clicking on the

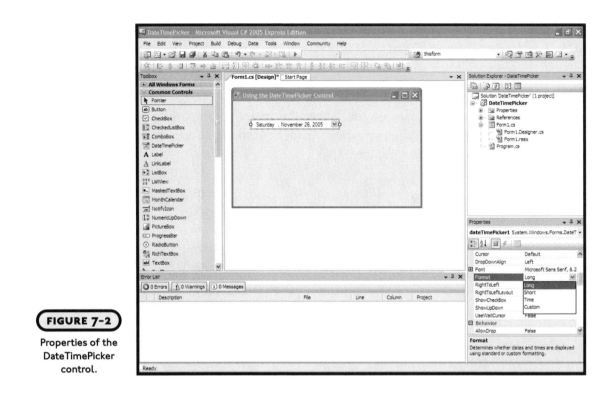

FIGURE 7-2

Properties of the
DateTimePicker
control.

arrow displays the calendar for the current month, as shown in Figure 7-3. A user can navigate to previous and future months and can select a date by clicking on it. After the user
clicks on a date, the calendar closes, and the date is displayed by the DateTimePicker control. The Value property gives us access via code to the selected date:

```
string CurrentDate = DTPcontrol.Value;
```

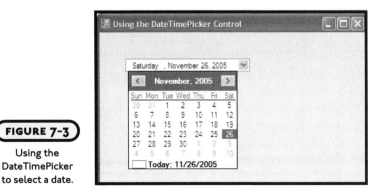

FIGURE 7-3

Using the
DateTimePicker
to select a date.

It is really quite easy to insert a control on a form. In this chapter, we will explore a variety of the controls available in Visual C# 2005 Express, such as timers, tabs, menus and toolbars.

THE TIMER CONTROL

The Timer control is used to execute code at regular intervals. The user cannot view or interact with the Timer control. When you drag a Timer control onto a form, it is placed within the gray area below a form (see Figure 7-4).

The Timer control, unlike other controls, has very few properties (see Figure 7-4). The Enabled property must be set to True for the Timer control to trigger code. The Interval property specifies how often the Timer control needs to trigger an event. It is set in milliseconds; 1000 milliseconds is equal to 1 second.

The following exercise shows how to use the Timer control to create a digital clock:

1. Create a new Windows Forms application called DigitalClock.

2. Set the Text property of the form to Digital Clock.

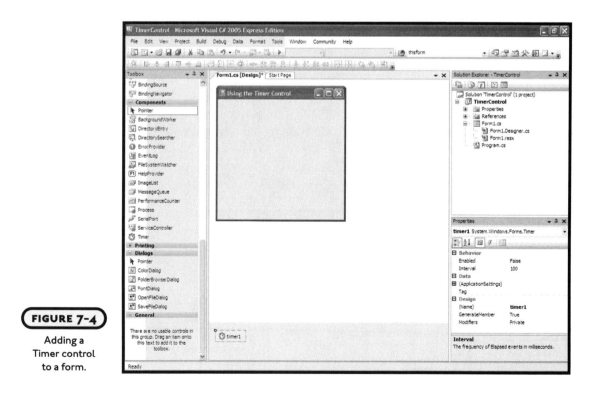

FIGURE 7-4

Adding a
Timer control
to a form.

3. Drag a Label control onto the form. Set the Name property of the control to **Clock**.

4. Drag a Timer control onto the form. The Timer control is located in the Components section of the Toolbox. The Timer control is added to the gray panel below the form.

5. Set the Enabled property of the Timer control to True.

6. Set the Interval property to 1000. This is 1000 milliseconds.

7. Double-click on the Timer control. A Tick method will be created for the Timer control. The Tick method is executed at each interval.

8. To get the current time and then update the Label control, enter the following code:

```
clock.Text = DateTime.Now.ToLongTimeString();
clock.Text = DateTime.Now.ToLongTimeString();
```

9. Press F5 to run the application. Voilà! A digital clock with second precision (see Figure 7-5).

FIGURE 7-5

The digital clock.

TABBED DIALOG BOXES

What do you do when a form requires so many controls that the interface no longer fits on a single screen? The solution is to group the controls by functionality and place them on separate tabs (see Figure 7-6). Tabs save space and make applications more usable. Tabs are also easy to implement, thanks to Visual C# 2005 Express Edition.

When a Tab control is added to a form, it has only two tabs. We can add more tabs to the TabPages collection by selecting the TabPage property and then clicking on the small button with three dots (also known as the Build button) that appears. This launches the Tab-Page Collection Editor, shown in Figure 7-7. Within the TabPage Collection Editor, we can add, remove, reorder, and set the properties on individual tabs. Each tab is named tabPage with a unique number postfixed to the end, such as tabPage1. The Text property sets the title that is actually displayed on the tab. Each tab is a container, so other controls can be dragged onto and grouped within tabs.

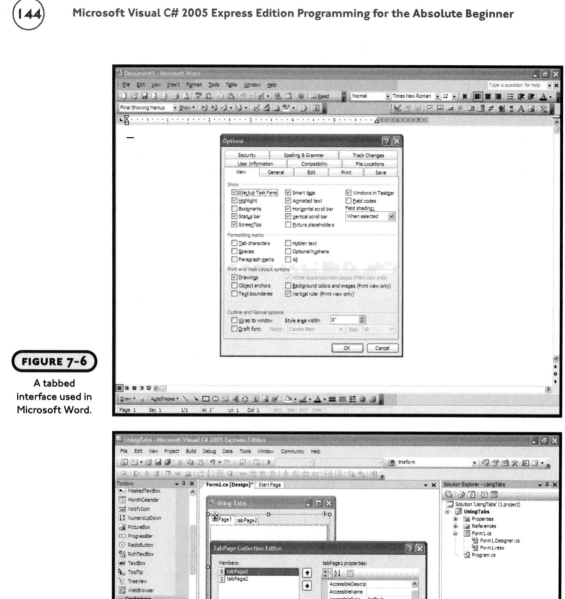

FIGURE 7-6

A tabbed interface used in Microsoft Word.

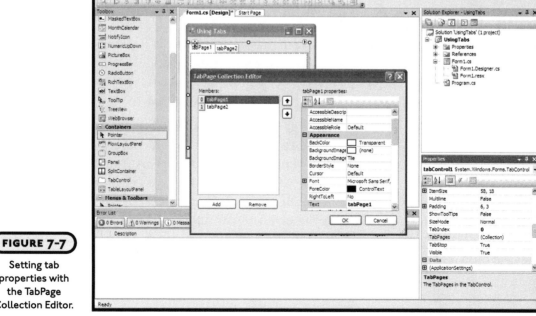

FIGURE 7-7

Setting tab properties with the TabPage Collection Editor.

THE TREEVIEW CONTROL

The TreeView control displays expandable hierarchical lists. This could be either an organizational chart or a list of the files and directories located on your hard drive, similar to Windows Explorer.

Items in a TreeView control are called nodes. No nodes are displayed when a TreeView control is first added to a form. We can add items to the node collection by selecting the Nodes property and then clicking on the Build button. This launches the TreeNode Editor, shown in Figure 7-8, within which we can add a root, nodes (parents), and subnodes (children). We can also set properties for each node.

The TreeView control can also be manipulated by C# code. This provides us with an enormous amount of flexibility. We can now build dynamic applications that deal with hierarchical lists.

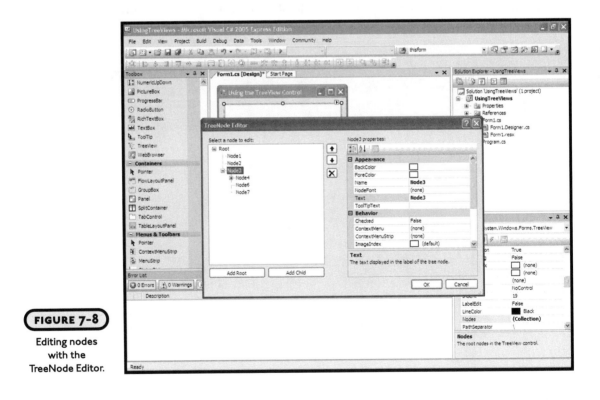

FIGURE 7-8

Editing nodes with the TreeNode Editor.

The following is the C# code that you use to add a node:

```
treeVW.Nodes.Add("Node 1");
To add a subnode, use the following:
TreeNode objNode;
objNode = treeVW.Nodes.Add("Node 1");
objNode.Nodes.Add("Node 1.1");
```

Removing the selected node and all of its child nodes is accomplished as follows:

```
treeVW.Nodes.Remove(treeVW.SelectedNode);
```

ADDING A MENU

A menu provides a convenient way to access all the functionality contained within an application. Common menus found in many applications include File, Edit, and Help. The File menu, shown in Figure 7-9, is a good example of a menu that is commonly found in applications; it includes commands that allow you to open, save, and exit an application.

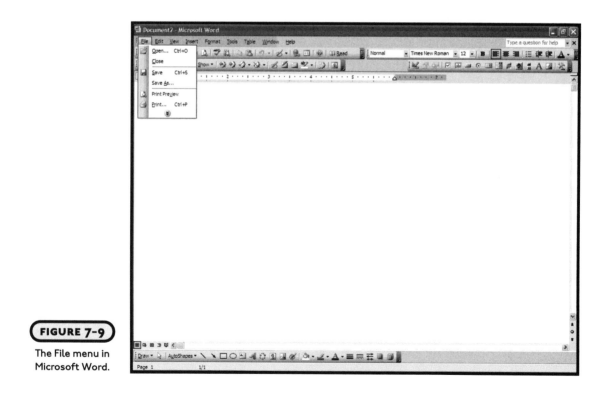

FIGURE 7-9

The File menu in
Microsoft Word.

The MenuStrip control, when added, is placed at the top of the form and within the gray area below a form. At the top of the form, you will see the text "Type Here" (see Figure 7-10).

Click on the Type Here text and replace it with File. This creates a File menu. Two new boxes are displayed below and to the left of the File menu. Both boxes display the Type Here text. Changing the Type Here text below the File menu creates a submenu item within the File menu. Replacing the Type Here text to the left of the File menu creates a new menu. Every time you change the Type Here text, you get the opportunity to add more menu items below and to the left of it.

As you can see in Figure 7-11, it is very easy to create a complex menu. If you want to remove an item from the menu, simply right-click on the menu item and click on Delete.

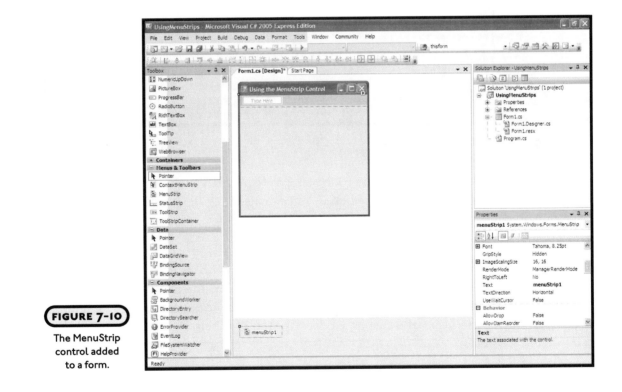

FIGURE 7-10

The MenuStrip control added to a form.

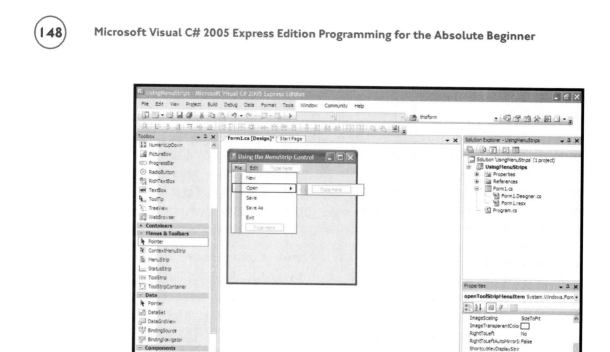

Creating a menu.

If you double-click on a menu item, the code panel is displayed, in which you can add code that will be executed when the item is clicked. You can also drag items to a new location on the menu, if you need to reorganize the menu.

THE TOOLSTRIP CONTROL

The ToolStrip control displays a group of buttons directly below the menu (see Figure 7-12). The toolbar is always visible and usually contains buttons to access frequently used application features. Each button also displays a ToolTip. ToolTips help a user to figure out the purpose of each button.

The ToolStrip control is added to the top of the form, but below a MenuStrip control. Select the ToolStrip control. You'll see a drop-down box that lists the type of controls that can be added to a ToolStrip. Select the Button control from the drop-down list (see Figure 7.13). A Button control will be added to the ToolStrip. You can drag buttons on a ToolStrip control to new locations, as well as delete them. Again, you can double-click on a button to add code to its Click event.

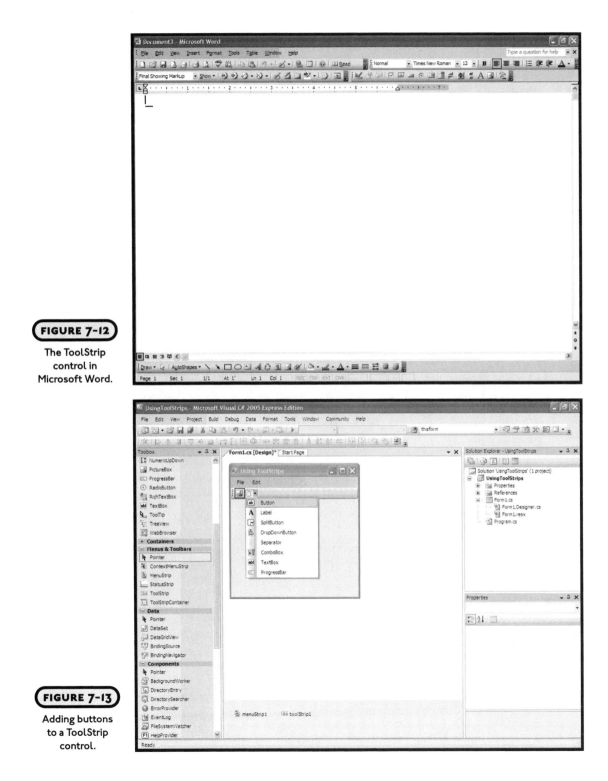

FIGURE 7-12

The ToolStrip control in Microsoft Word.

FIGURE 7-13

Adding buttons to a ToolStrip control.

BACK TO THE SHARP PAINTING APPLICATION

The Sharp Painting application gives us the opportunity to build an application that has a menu and a ToolStrip control. The application enables a user to select a shape type and then use the mouse to draw the shape onto the applications form. You will need to use the graphics programming techniques that you learned in Chapter 6.

Designing the Interface

Figure 7-14 illustrates the interface that our application will use. The interface has a menu and a ToolStrip control. The ToolStrip control contains two buttons that enable the user to select whether they would like to draw a line or a rectangle. The MenuStrip control has File and Draw menus. The File menu has New and Exit items. The New menu item simply clears all shapes drawn by the user. The Exit menu item closes the application. The Draw menu contains items that correspond to the features available on the ToolStrip control; these allow the user to specify whether a rectangle or a line should be drawn.

FIGURE 7-14

The Sharp Painting application.

Building the SharpPainting interface:

1. Create a new Windows Forms application called SharpPainting.

2. Change the Text property of the form to Sharp Painting. This changes the text that is displayed on the title bar of the form.

3. Add a MenuStrip control to the form.

4. At the top of the form, click on the text Type Here and type **File**. The File menu is created.

5. Click on the Type Here text displayed below the File menu and type **New** to create the New menu item.

6. Click on the Type Here text displayed below the New menu and type **Exit** to create the Exit menu.

7. Click on the Type Here text next to the File menu and type **Draw** to create the Draw menu.

8. Click on the Type Here text displayed below the Rectangle menu item and type **Line** to create the Circle menu.

9. Click on the Type Here text below the Draw menu and type **Rectangle** to create the Rectangle menu item.

10. Drag a ToolStrip control onto the form.

11. Click on the ToolStrip; this will select it. You'll see the drop-down box. Select the Button control from the drop-down list. A Button control will be added to the ToolStrip. Set the Name of the Button to LineButton. Set the DisplayStyle property to Text. Set the Text property to Line. The New button is added to the ToolStrip.

12. A drop-down box is displayed next to the Line button. Add the Rectangle button to the ToolStrip. Set the Name of the Button to RectangleButton. Set the DisplayStyle property to Text. Set the Text property to Rectangle.

Programming the C# Code

The important question becomes, how does the user use the mouse to draw a shape? We want the user to click and hold down the left mouse button at the start position, continue to drag the mouse, and finally release the mouse button when the required size of the shape is reached. We will need to capture MouseDown, MouseUp, and MouseMove events. The MouseDown event needs to set the starting x and y positions of the shape. The MouseMove event must draw a preview of the shape. When the MouseUp event is fired, we need to get the end x and y position and finally draw the shape onto the canvas.

Writing the C# code for the SharpPainting application:

1. Enter the following code to create some variables to store a Rectangle object, the start and end coordinates, and the selected shape:

```
using System;
using System.Collections.Generic;
using System.ComponentModel;
using System.Data;
using System.Drawing;
using System.Text;
using System.Windows.Forms;

namespace SharpPainting
{
    public partial class Form1 : Form
    {
        Rectangle SelectionRectangle = new Rectangle();
        Point StartPoint = new Point();
        Point EndPoint = new Point();
        string SelectedShape = "Rectangle";

        public Form1()
        {
        }

        public void OnMouseDown_Handler(Object sender, MouseEventArgs e)
        {
        }

        public void OnMouseMove_Handler(Object sender, MouseEventArgs e)
        {
        }
        public void OnMouseUp_Handler(Object sender, MouseEventArgs e)
```

```
            {
            }
            private void RectangleButton_Click(object sender, EventArgs e)
            {
            }
            private void LineButton_Click(object sender, EventArgs e)
            {
            }
            private void lineToolStripMenuItem_Click(object sender, EventArgs
    e)
            {
            }
            private void rectangleToolStripMenuItem_Click(object sender,
    EventArgs e)
            {
            }
            private void newToolStripMenuItem_Click(object sender, EventArgs e)
            {
            }
            private void exitToolStripMenuItem_Click(object sender, EventArgs
    e)
            {
            }
        }
    }
```

2. Add event handlers for the MouseUp, MouseDown, and MouseMove events by entering the following code within the form's constructor method:

```
public Form1()
        {
                InitializeComponent();
                this.MouseDown += new MouseEventHandler(OnMouseDown_Handler);
                this.MouseMove += new MouseEventHandler(OnMouseMove_Handler);
                this.MouseUp += new MouseEventHandler(OnMouseUp_Handler);
        }
```

3. Add the following code so that the OnMouseDown event handler can capture the starting coordinates and reset our selection rectangle:

```
public void OnMouseDown_Handler(Object sender, MouseEventArgs e)
{
        SelectionRectangle.Width = 0;
        SelectionRectangle.Height = 0;
        SelectionRectangle.X = e.X;
        SelectionRectangle.Y = e.Y;

        StartPoint.X = e.X;
        StartPoint.Y = e.Y;
        EndPoint = StartPoint;
}
```

4. Add the following code so that the OnMouseMove event handler draws a preview of the shape while the left mouse button is down:

```
public void OnMouseMove_Handler(Object sender, MouseEventArgs e)
        {
                if (e.Button == MouseButtons.Left)
                {
                        Form CurrentForm = (Form)sender;
                        if (SelectedShape == "Line")
                        {

ControlPaint.DrawReversibleLine(CurrentForm.PointToScreen(StartPoint),
CurrentForm.PointToScreen(EndPoint), Color.Black);
                                EndPoint = new Point(e.X, e.Y);

ControlPaint.DrawReversibleLine(CurrentForm.PointToScreen(StartPoint),
CurrentForm.PointToScreen(EndPoint), Color.Black);
                        }
                        else if (SelectedShape == "Rectangle")
                        {
ControlPaint.DrawReversibleFrame(CurrentForm.RectangleToScreen(SelectionRectangle
), Color.Black, FrameStyle.Dashed);
                                SelectionRectangle.Width = e.X -
SelectionRectangle.X;
```

```
                                   SelectionRectangle.Height = e.Y -
SelectionRectangle.Y;
ControlPaint.DrawReversibleFrame(CurrentForm.RectangleToScreen(SelectionRectangle
), Color.Black, FrameStyle.Dashed);
                    }
                }
            }
```

5. Add the following code so that the OnMouseUp event handler can capture the end coordinates of the shape and draw the appropriate shape on the form:

```
            public void OnMouseUp_Handler(Object sender, MouseEventArgs e)
            {
                    Form CurrentForm = (Form)sender;
                    Graphics g = CurrentForm.CreateGraphics();
                    Pen pen = new Pen(Color.Blue, 2);
                    if (SelectedShape == "Line")
                    {
ControlPaint.DrawReversibleLine(CurrentForm.PointToScreen(StartPoint),
CurrentForm.PointToScreen(EndPoint), Color.Black);
                            g.DrawLine(pen, StartPoint, EndPoint);
                    }
                    else if (SelectedShape == "Rectangle")
                    {
ControlPaint.DrawReversibleFrame(CurrentForm.RectangleToScreen(SelectionRectangle
), Color.Black, FrameStyle.Dashed);
                            g.DrawRectangle(pen, SelectionRectangle);
                    }
                    g.Dispose();
            }
```

6. Double-click on each of the ToolStrip control buttons to enter code to assign the appropriate shape to the ShapeToDraw variable:

```
            private void RectangleButton_Click(object sender, EventArgs e)
            {
                    SelectedShape = "Rectangle";
            }
            private void LineButton_Click(object sender, EventArgs e)
            {
```

```
                    SelectedShape = "Line";
        }
```

7. Double-click on each of the MenuStrip control buttons to enter code to assign the appropriate shape to the `ShapeToDraw` variable:

```
        private void lineToolStripMenuItem_Click(object sender, EventArgs e)
        {
                SelectedShape = "Line";
        }
        private void rectangleToolStripMenuItem_Click(object sender,
EventArgs e)
        {
                SelectedShape = "Rectangle";
        }
```

8. Finally, we need to add code to clear and close the form.

```
        private void newToolStripMenuItem_Click(object sender, EventArgs e)
        {
                Invalidate();
        }
        private void exitToolStripMenuItem_Click(object sender, EventArgs e)
        {
                this.Close();
        }
```

The full code listing:

```
using System;
using System.Collections.Generic;
using System.ComponentModel;
using System.Data;
using System.Drawing;
using System.Text;
using System.Windows.Forms;

namespace SharpPainting
```

```
{

    public partial class Form1 : Form
    {
        Rectangle SelectionRectangle = new Rectangle();
        Point StartPoint = new Point();
        Point EndPoint = new Point();
        string SelectedShape = "Rectangle";

        public Form1()
        {
            InitializeComponent();
            this.MouseDown += new MouseEventHandler(OnMouseDown_Handler);
            this.MouseMove += new MouseEventHandler(OnMouseMove_Handler);
            this.MouseUp += new MouseEventHandler(OnMouseUp_Handler);
        }

        public void OnMouseDown_Handler(Object sender, MouseEventArgs e)
        {
            SelectionRectangle.Width = 0;
            SelectionRectangle.Height = 0;
            SelectionRectangle.X = e.X;
            SelectionRectangle.Y = e.Y;

            StartPoint.X = e.X;
            StartPoint.Y = e.Y;
            EndPoint = StartPoint;
        }

        public void OnMouseMove_Handler(Object sender, MouseEventArgs e)
        {
            if (e.Button == MouseButtons.Left)
            {
                Form CurrentForm = (Form)sender;
                if (SelectedShape == "Line")
                {
```

ControlPaint.DrawReversibleLine(CurrentForm.PointToScreen(StartPoint),
CurrentForm.PointToScreen(EndPoint), Color.Black);

```
                    EndPoint = new Point(e.X, e.Y);

ControlPaint.DrawReversibleLine(CurrentForm.PointToScreen(StartPoint),
CurrentForm.PointToScreen(EndPoint), Color.Black);
                }
                else if (SelectedShape == "Rectangle")
                {
ControlPaint.DrawReversibleFrame(CurrentForm.RectangleToScreen(SelectionRectangle
), Color.Black, FrameStyle.Dashed);
                    SelectionRectangle.Width = e.X -
SelectionRectangle.X;
                    SelectionRectangle.Height = e.Y -
SelectionRectangle.Y;
ControlPaint.DrawReversibleFrame(CurrentForm.RectangleToScreen(SelectionRectangle
), Color.Black, FrameStyle.Dashed);
                }
            }
        }
        public void OnMouseUp_Handler(Object sender, MouseEventArgs e)
        {
            Form CurrentForm = (Form)sender;
            Graphics g = CurrentForm.CreateGraphics();
            Pen pen = new Pen(Color.Blue, 2);
            if (SelectedShape == "Line")
            {
ControlPaint.DrawReversibleLine(CurrentForm.PointToScreen(StartPoint),
CurrentForm.PointToScreen(EndPoint), Color.Black);
                g.DrawLine(pen, StartPoint, EndPoint);
            }
            else if (SelectedShape == "Rectangle")
            {
ControlPaint.DrawReversibleFrame(CurrentForm.RectangleToScreen(SelectionRectangle
), Color.Black, FrameStyle.Dashed);
                g.DrawRectangle(pen, SelectionRectangle);
            }
            g.Dispose();
        }
```

```
        private void RectangleButton_Click(object sender, EventArgs e)
        {
                SelectedShape = "Rectangle";
        }
        private void LineButton_Click(object sender, EventArgs e)
        {
                SelectedShape = "Line";
        }
        private void lineToolStripMenuItem_Click(object sender, EventArgs
    e)

        {
                SelectedShape = "Line";
        }
        private void rectangleToolStripMenuItem_Click(object sender,
    EventArgs e)
        {
                SelectedShape = "Rectangle";
        }
        private void newToolStripMenuItem_Click(object sender, EventArgs e)
        {
                Invalidate();
        }
        private void exitToolStripMenuItem_Click(object sender, EventArgs
    e)

        {
                this.Close();
        }
    }
}
```

Testing the Application

Very cool! You have just created a user-friendly drawing application, complete with a menu and toolbar. Test the application by trying to draw some simple shapes. If all appears to be working well, then move on to drawing simple objects like a house or television set. Sharp Painting has many limitations. These are not bugs, but just features that need to be implemented before Sharp Painting is a complete drawing package. Try to complete the tasks in the "Challenges" section to enhance the drawing application.

Summary

I'm sure you'll agree that interface layout and design are simple tasks when you are using Visual C# 2005 Express Edition. Adding an interface control involves dragging a control onto a form, setting its properties, and writing code to respond to events, such as a click. This chapter covered some advanced controls, such as Tab, Timer, Menu, TreeView, and ToolStrip controls. Have fun with the new controls in your toolkit as you build functional, user-friendly applications. The possibilities are endless.

Challenges

1. Create an image slideshow viewer. You will need to use the Timer and PictureBox controls.

2. Use a TreeView control to create a To Do List application.

3. Use the CheckBoxList and ListView controls in an application.

4. Enhance the Sharp Painting application by allowing the user to specify colors, draw filled objects, draw additional shapes, and print drawings. You will need to do some research to add all of these features.

OBJECT-ORIENTED PROGRAMMING FOR THE ABSOLUTE BEGINNER

O bject-oriented programming is not difficult. It actually provides a very natural and intuitive model for structuring and organizing program- ming code. C# is a very powerful object-oriented language, but it is still well suited for a beginning programmer. Object-oriented programming groups together data and the methods that access and modify the data. Object-oriented code is easier to modify, maintain, enhance, and reuse. Object-oriented pro- gramming makes it easy to model real-world applications in programming code. In this chapter you will learn how to:

- Model objects in C# code.
- Declare instance variables.
- Declare methods.
- Overload methods.
- Implement inheritance.

WHAT IS OBJECT-ORIENTED PROGRAMMING?

The usefulness of object-oriented programming becomes evident only when compared with procedural programming, which was very linear. Lots of variables and functions (also known as methods) were mixed together. This approach simply did not work for large, complex software systems. As you can imagine, figuring out which methods changed which data was difficult. Procedural programs are not only hard to maintain and enhance they also make identifying and fixing bugs difficult. Enhancements also usually lead to more bugs, because it was hard to identify dependencies. To sum up it, the life of a programmer was much more stressful before object-oriented programming came to the rescue.

Object-oriented programming introduces a new concept: the object. An object is a real-world entity that has attributes and behaviors. An object groups together the characteristics that describe an object (properties) and the things that the object can do or have done to it via methods.

This is all going to make much more sense after we look at a few practical examples. Our first example explores a Car object.

A car has the following characteristics, properties, or attributes:

- Make
- Model
- Color

Things we can do while driving a car are known as behaviors or methods. We can also do the following things while driving the car:

- Brake()
- Accelerate()
- TurnLeft()
- TurnRight()
- Reverse()

Creating a Car object has allowed us to group together associated properties and methods, a procedure known as *encapsulation*. We can now create our own Car instance objects, after which we can immediately see the properties and methods that are available. As you can imagine, a complex application would comprise many objects. Without object-oriented concepts, it would be hard to expose the functionality defined by each object or item within a system.

Another example of an object is a Windows Forms interface element such as a button. We have used a button in almost every chapter of this book. We usually drag a button onto a form and set its attributes within the Properties explorer. There are also methods such as the OnClick event handler that are associated with the button control. The Properties window makes it very easy to expose for viewing all the available functionality within an object. Programming would be much harder without the methods and properties of interface elements being encapsulated.

Another object-oriented concept is polymorphism (Greek for multiple forms). Polymorphism allows the same function to accept different parameters. This means that you can declare methods with the same name multiple times, with each method accepting a different number of parameters or arguments, as well as parameters of a different data type. This capability is very powerful. The Response.Write() method is an excellent example of how polymorphism works. This method prints data of any type (integer, string, or Boolean value) to a Web page. No matter what the data type is, we can use the same method. It would be very confusing if we had to use the Response.WriteInt() method to print an integer, use the Response.WriteString() method to print text, and so forth. Remembering and using only one method is much easier than remembering and using many methods.

Inheritance is another feature of object-oriented programming. Inheritance enables us to reuse and extend existing objects. A parent object defines the base or generic properties and methods. Child objects can then inherit functionality from their parent. An example would be a generic object to model pets. This would describe only those features and behaviors that are common to all pets. A child object, such as a dog object, could then inherit from the pet object and also incorporate its own properties and behaviors. Inheritance essentially establishes an object hierarchy.

CLASSES AND OBJECTS

Enough theory! I bet you are wondering how we define an object and then create object instances in C#. Obviously, we have to group the properties and methods together. A class is the programming construct in C# that allows us to achieve this.

As an example, the following is the class to define car objects:

```
public class Car
{
        string Make
        string Model
        string Color
```

```
    public Brake()
    {

    }

    public Accelerate()
    {

    }

    public TurnLeft()
    {

    }

    public TurnRight()
    {

    }

    public Reverse()
    {

    }
}
```

Variables contained within a class are known as data members, properties, or fields. An instance of these variables is created every time a new object is created. Each object instance is able to have its own data stored within these variables.

We place within methods the code that can manipulate properties, as well as implement the behaviors of the object. Methods access the instance variables stored for each unique object.

The following is the basic syntax to create a class in C#:

```
modifier_type class classname
{
        modifier_type data_type variable_name;
```

```
public classname()
{
      // insert code initialize object
}

modifier_type data_type method_name (parameter1, parameter2, ....,parameterN)
{
      // insert method code here
}
}
```

When you are implementing a class, keep the following points in mind:

- The class access modifier, which is usually public, defines access to the class. The public access modifier makes the class visible to all other classes.
- The class keyword follows the access modifier.
- The name of the class follows the class keyword.
- Properties and methods in a class are placed within a code block, i.e., { and }.
- Properties must be declared.
- Access modifiers, such as private and public, can precede the data type when declaring a property. The private modifier only allows methods within its own class to access it. Use the public modifier to make the property accessible from code outside the class.
- A method can also have a type modifier, such as private or public.
- A method can have a return data type, such as an int or string. This defines the type of data a method returns after it is called. A method that does not return data needs the void data type.
- Parameters passed to the method must be separated by a comma.

CREATING AN EMPLOYEE CLASS

The example that follows models an Employee as an object. The Employee class needs properties to store the name and e-mail address of an employee. The class has a method to display the employee details.

For this example, we need to do the following:

1. Declare a public class called Employee.

2. Declare the name variable as a string.

3. Declare the e-mail variable as a string.

4. Declare a public method called DisplayEmployee that returns a string data type.

5. The return keyword will need to be used within the method to return the data.

This is what the actual class looks like in C#:

```
public class Employee
{
        public string name();
        public string email;
        public string displayEmployee()
        {
        return (name + " (" + email + ")";
        }
}
```

We can then create Employee objects and set object properties. The new keyword is used to create an object instance from a class definition, which is what the following code does:

```
Employee employee1 = new Employee();
employee1.name = "Aneesha";
employee1.email="a.b@codeintime.com";
We can also call the displayEmployee() method:
Employee1.DisplayEmployee();
We can also create any number of objects, such as these:
Employee employee1 = new Employee();
employee1.name = "Aneesha";
employee1.email="a.b@codeintime.com";

Employee employee2 = new Employee();
Employee2.name = "Zaeem";
Employee2.email="z.b@codeintime.com";
```

```
Employee employee3 = new Employee();
Employee3.name = "Celine";
Employee3.email="c.b@codeintime.com";
```

CONSTRUCTORS

Constructors are special methods that we can execute and pass parameters to when we initialize an object. Code within a constructor is executed each time the class is instantiated. This is an ideal place to insert code that must be run once when an object is created. We can use a constructor to initialize an object's properties when the object is created. The constructor method is named after the class. The constructor for the Employee class follows:

```
public class Employee
{
      public string name;
      public string email;

      public Employee(string e_name, string e_email)
      {
            name = e_name;
            email = e_email;
      }
      public string displayEmployee()
      {
            return (name + " (" + email + ")");
      }
}
```

We can now initialize our Employee objects with a single line of code:

```
Employee employee1 = new Employee("Aneesha","a.b@codeintime.com");
Employee employee2 = new Employee("Zaeem","z.b@codeintime.com");
Employee employee3 = new Employee("Celine","c.b@codeintime.com");
```

STATIC VARIABLES

Static variables store data that needs to be common to all objects. Static variables are the same for each instantiated object. We could use a static variable to keep a running count of all objects created. A static variable is preceded by the static keyword.

The Employee class:

```
public class Employee
{
      public string name;
      public string email;
      static public int employee_count;

      public Employee(string e_name, string e_email)
      {
            name = e_name;
            email - e_email;
            employee_count++;
      }

      public string displayEmployee()
      {
            return (name + " (" + email + ")";
      }
}
```

The employee_count variable can be accessed as a class property:

```
int no_of_employees = Employee.employee_count;
```

OVERLOADED METHODS

As previously stated, polymorphism allows methods with the same name to accept a varying number of parameters, as well as parameters of different data types. C# compares the parameters passed with the parameter signatures for each of the methods in the class and executes the matching method. Even constructors can be overloaded.

In the following example, the CalculateSalary() method is overloaded. If a single parameter is passed to it, the CalculateSalary(double hrsRate) method is executed. If two parameters are passed to it, the CalculateSalary(double hrsRate, double hrsWorked) method is executed.

```
public class Employee
{
      public string name;
      public string email;
      public double hourlyRate=25;
```

```
    public double hoursWorked=36.5;

    public Employee(string e_name, string e_email)
    {
        name = e_name;
        email = e_email;
    }

    public double CalculateSalary(double hrsRate)
    {
        return (hrsRate * hoursWorked);
    }

    public double CalculateSalary(double hrsRate, double hrsWorked)
    {
        return (hrsRate * hrsWorked);
    }
}
```

CREATING PROPERTIES

A property is an instance variable that has special methods that can set and retrieve its data. Properties restrict access to instance variables. Properties allow us to hide the internal workings of a class and make future enhancements or modifications without affecting the code that uses the objects. Properties have get and set code blocks that are executed when a value is assigned or retrieved. We could, for example, perform validation before a value is assigned to an instance variable.

The following class includes get and set code blocks for the name and e-mail instance variables within the Employee class:

```
public class Employee
{
    private string emp_name;
    private string emp_email;

    public string name
    {
        get
```

```
                {
                        return emp_name;
                }
                set
                {
                        return emp_email;
                }
        }

        public string email
        {
                get
                {
                        return emp_email;
                }
                set
                {
                        return emp_email;
                }
        }
}
```

In summary, a property is created by doing the following:

1. Declaring a public variable.

2. Inserting a code block after the variable name.

3. Inserting a get code block (the final line of the get code block must use the return keyword to send back the value of the property).

4. Inserting a set code block (the final line of the set code block must set the value of a hidden instance variable).

USING NAMESPACES

A namespace is used to group a collection of related classes. It is possible for class name conflicts to occur, especially when you start incorporating open-source or commercial classes within your application. A namespace helps to solve this problem. It is considered good practice to place all the classes of an application within a namespace. Visual C# Express automatically does this for all classes contained within a project, an example of which is shown in Figure 8-1.

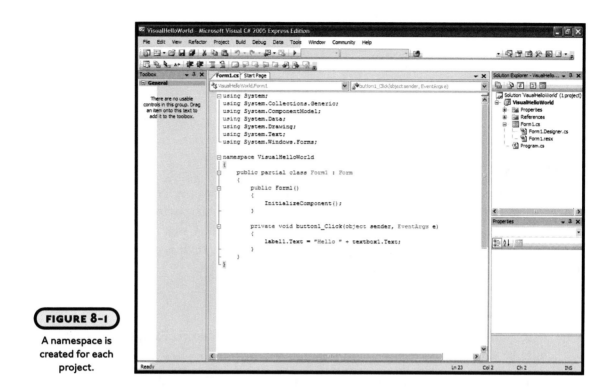

FIGURE 8-1

A namespace is
created for each
project.

The namespace keyword is used to define a namespace:

```
namespace Employee
{
    public class Employee
    {
        public string name;
        public string email;
        static public int employee_count;

        public Employee(string e_name, string e_email)
        {
            name = e_name;
            email = e_email;
            employee_count++;
        }
```

```
        public string displayEmployee()
        {
                return (name + " (" + email + ")");
        }
    }
}
```

SUMMARY

A lot of theory on object-oriented programming techniques has been covered in this chapter. We first looked at three important characteristics of object-oriented programming: encapsulation, inheritance, and polymorphism. The class in C# was also introduced as a blueprint for creating object instances. Object-oriented terms, such as properties, constructors, overloaded methods, and namespaces, were also explained.

CHALLENGES

1. Design and build an object-oriented application of your choice. Example applications could be a quiz, a game, or a business application.

2. Build an interface for, and enhance, the Employee class. You need to allow the user to add, edit, and display employee details.

WORKING WITH DATABASES

atabases provide a simple way to store and retrieve structured data in a multiuser environment. It is much easier to design, store, and retrieve data within a database than it is to design a custom file format for your application. Using databases in your applications and projects will save you heaps of time. Almost every Web site that you encounter while surfing the Internet uses a database. In this chapter you will learn how to:

- Create a database in Microsoft Access.
- Write simple database queries.
- Create a database connection.
- Display editable database records with a DataGridView control.
- Bind data retrieved from a database to form controls, such as TextBox and Label controls.
- Design and code the Guess A Word game, which uses a database to store words and their associated clues.

PROJECT PREVIEW: THE GUESS A WORD GAME

In the Guess A Word game, shown in Figure 9-1, the player is provided with a clue and has to guess the associated word, concept, activity, or object. Pretty simple really! There is a catch—all the words and clues must be retrieved from a Microsoft Access database. Don't worry, though, because we will first cover the basics of database design and the retrieval of data from a database. When it is time to build this project toward the end of the chapter, you'll have all the confidence and skill needed to make the project a success.

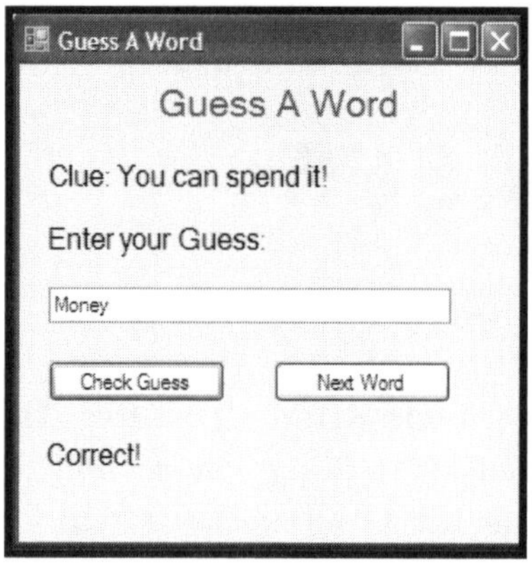

FIGURE 9-1

Playing the Guess A Word game.

WHAT IS A DATABASE?

A database stores structured data—rows and rows of structured data in multiple tables. A database is best explained with an example. A simple database that we could build is an employee database. The purpose of this database is to store the details of everybody who works for a company.

We start by making a list of all the details we need to collect. This includes:

- An employee ID that is unique, meaning that no two employees can have the same ID
- First name
- Surname or last name
- E-mail address
- Phone extension
- Role or position within the company
- Department

We need to store these details for each employee within the company. The best way to collate and display the data that we need to store is with a table. Each row within the table represents an employee. The columns store the details we need to collect for each user. Columns are known as database fields. Table 9-1 illustrates our example EmployeeDetails table with four employee records.

TABLE 9-1 EMPLOYEEDETAILS TABLE

ID	First Name	Surname	E-mail	Phone Ext.	Role	Department
1	Aneesha	Bakharia	a.b@codeintime.com	0934	Programmer	R&D
2	Zaeem	Bakharia	z.b@codeintime.com	2345	Programmer	R&D
3	Celine	Bakharia	c.b@codeintime.com	3456	Designer	R&D
4	Tess	Bakharia	t.b@codeintime.com	4567	Project Manager	HR

We can edit the details stored in the table, delete entire records, and add new records. Table 9-1 is a single table within a database. However, a database can have many tables. There can even be relationships between tables. Why do we need relationships between tables? Take a look at the EmployeeDetails table. The Department field or column has repeated data because we have three employees within the R&D department. What if the R&D department changed its name? We'd have to go and update each record individually. We could use a search and replace operation, but this still involves making a change to each record. Surely there must be an easier way.

Indeed, there is a simple solution. We need to create a new table called Departments. This table needs three fields or columns: DepartmentID, Department, and Description. We then only need to store the DepartmentID within the EmployeeDetails table (see Table 9-2). This field is related to the Departments table (see Table 9-3). We need to update a department's name in only one place. This is known as referential integrity.

That's enough on databases to whet your appetite. This has been a very basic introduction to databases—just enough for you to create a database and build a simple application that uses a database in Visual C# 2005 Express Edition. If you are interested in more information, there are entire books dedicated to relational databases.

TABLE 9-2 THE EMPLOYEEDETAILS TABLE

ID	First Name	Surname	E-mail	Phone Ext.	Role	DepartmentID
1	Aneesha	Bakharia	a.b@codeintime.com	0934	Programmer	1
2	Zaeem	Bakharia	z.b@codeintime.com	2345	Programmer	1
3	Celine	Bakharia	c.b@codeintime.com	3456	Designer	1
4	Tess	Bakharia	t.b@codeintime.com	4567	Project Manager	2

TABLE 9-3 DEPARTMENTS TABLE

DepartmentID	Department	Description
1	R&D	Research and Development
2	HR	Human Resources

CREATING A DATABASE WITH MICROSOFT ACCESS

Microsoft Access is a relational database development software tool that is part of Microsoft Office, but it can also be purchased separately. If you have never created a database, Microsoft Access (see Figure 9-2) is the perfect tool for you. It is both easy to use and feature rich. As you progress and start to build applications that are used by hundreds of users simultaneously, you will have to step up to Microsoft SQL Server or Microsoft SQL Server Express 2005. The database management concepts that you learn from implementing databases with Access are easily transferable to the higher-powered Microsoft SQL Server applications. We will only cover Microsoft Access in this chapter.

Within Access, we can create our EmployeeDetails and Departments tables, as well as define the relationships between these tables:

1. Open Microsoft Access from the Start menu.

2. Click on the Blank Database link. The File New Database dialog box opens.

3. Enter the database name, which in our case is EmployeeDatabase.

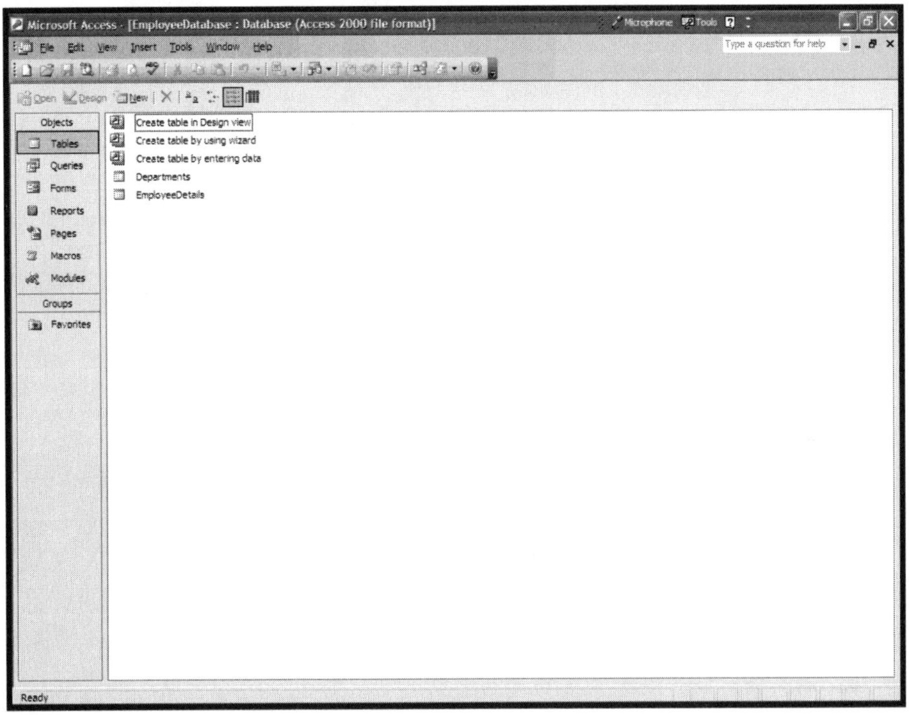

FIGURE 9-2

The Microsoft
Access
interface.

4. Click on Create. The database is created.

5. Click on the Tables tab and then click on New. The New Table dialog box opens.

6. Click on Design View. The option is selected.

7. Click on OK. The Table Design View window opens, as shown in Figure 9-3.

8. Type a field name in the Field Name column. The first field must be the primary key.

9. Click on the drop-down arrow of the Data Type column. All the types of data that can be stored in an Access database are displayed.

10. Click on AutoNumber. This option inserts a sequentially incremented number for each new record added. AutoNumber is unique for each record. This is what is required by a primary key.

11. Type in a description. This helps to identify the purpose and type of data being stored in a field.

12. Click on the Field Selection button. The field is selected.

13. Click on the Primary Key button. The selected field is converted into a primary key.

14. Type a field name in the Field Name column.

15. Click on the drop-down arrow of the Data Types column. All the types of data that can be stored in an Access database are displayed.

16. Click on the appropriate data type. The data type is selected. The following data types are available:

- **Text.** Holds up to 255 alphanumeric characters
- **Memo.** Stores large amounts of text
- **Number.** Stores numeric data
- **Data/Time.** Stores a date/time value
- **Currency.** Places a $ sign in front of a numeric value
- **Yes/No.** Stores a true or false, 1 or 0 value

17. Type in a description.

18. Repeat Steps 15 to 17 for each field in the EmployeeDetails table (see Figure 9-2).

19. Click on the Close icon. You are asked if you want to save the table.

20. Click on Yes. The Save As dialog box opens.

21. Type in the table name, which in our case is EmployeeDetails.

22. Click on OK. The table is saved.

23. Repeat Steps 6 to 22 for each table in the database. We need to create only one more table, called Departments (see Figure 9-3). Refer to Tables 9.2 and 9.3 for the column names.

24. Click on the Relationships button. The Show Table dialog box opens.

25. Ctrl+Click on the two tables we would like to create a relationship between. The tables are selected.

26. Click on Add. The tables are added to the Relationships window.

27. Click on Close. The Show Table dialog box closes.

28. Click on the field that you would like to link to another table. In our case, this is the DepartmentIDs field in the EmployeeDetails table.

29. Drag the field that you want to relate from one table to the related field in the other table. We want to drag from the DepartmentIDs field in the EmployeeDetails table to the DepartmentID field within the Departments table. The Edit Relationships dialog box opens.

30. Check the Enforce Referential Integrity check box.

31. Click on Create. A one-to-many relationship is created, and a line linking the two tables is drawn, as shown in Figure 9-4. This means that one record from the Departments table relates to many records within the EmployeeDetails table. We can also have one-to-one and many-to-many relationships.

32. Enter the data for the Departments table and then enter each employee's record within the EmployeeDetails table.

33. Click on the Close icon. Microsoft Access closes.

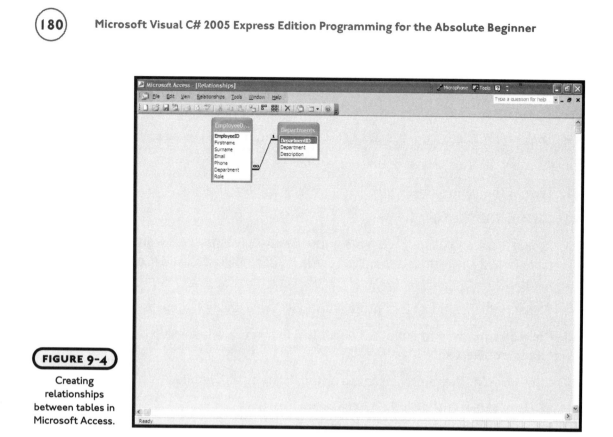

FIGURE 9-4

Creating
relationships
between tables in
Microsoft Access.

QUERYING A DATABASE

Lots and lots of data can be stored in a database. That is, after all, the purpose of a database. Our EmployeeDetails table could store four records, or if our company grows, it could store thousands of records. This raises an interesting question: How do we find data in a database? This is where the Structured Query Language (SQL) comes to our rescue. SQL enables us to retrieve the data we require from a database table or tables.

We use a Select statement to retrieve data from a table within a database:

```
SELECT * from tablename
```

The asterisk is a wildcard character and retrieves all records and all fields from the table.

So, if we want to retrieve all records from the EmployeeDetails table, the query would look like this:

```
SELECT * from EmployeeDetails
```

We can also only select specific fields for each record stored in the database:

```
SELECT fieldname1, fieldname2 , fieldname3 from tablename
```

If we only want an employee's surname and e-mail address, this is what the query would look like:

```
SELECT Surname, Email from EmployeeDetails
```

What if we do not want all records? We need to add criteria, which we do with the Where clause:

```
SELECT * from tablename WHERE fieldname1='value'
```

Let's retrieve all employees with Bakharia as their surname:

```
SELECT * from EmployeeDetails WHERE surname='Bakharia'
```

We can even combine criteria by using the AND and OR Boolean operators:

```
SELECT * from tablename WHERE fieldname1='value' AND fieldname2='value'
SELECT * from tablename WHERE fieldname1='value' OR fieldname2='value'
```

CREATING A DATABASE CONNECTION IN VISUAL C# 2005 EXPRESS EDITION

We have designed a database to store employee details, created the database in Microsoft Access, and learned how to write basic SQL queries to retrieve the data that we require. All that remains is to create an interface for our database in Visual C# 2005 Express Edition. Our first step is to create a database connection:

1. Create a new Windows Forms application called EmployeeDatabase.

2. Click on Data. The Data menu is displayed.

3. Click on Add New Data Source. The Data Source Configuration Wizard is displayed (see Figure 09-5).

4. Select Database and click on the Next button.

5. Click on the New Connection button. The Add Connection dialog box is displayed.

6. Change the Data Source to a Microsoft Access database. It is initially set to Microsoft SQL Server.

7. Browse for the EmployeeDatabase.mdb file we created in the previous section.

8. Click on the Test Connection button to ensure that connecting from Visual C# 2005 Express Edition works.

9. Click on OK. The Add Connection dialog box closes.

10. Click on the Next button. You are asked if you would like to copy the database to the current project folder.

11. Click on Yes and then on Next. The objects in your database including tables are displayed.

12. Expand the Tables node and select the EmployeeDetails and Departments tables.

13. Click on Finish. The Data Source Configuration Wizard finishes.

You'll notice that the database and a few files, such as EmployeeDatabaseDataSet.xsd, have been added to the Solution Explorer for the current project.

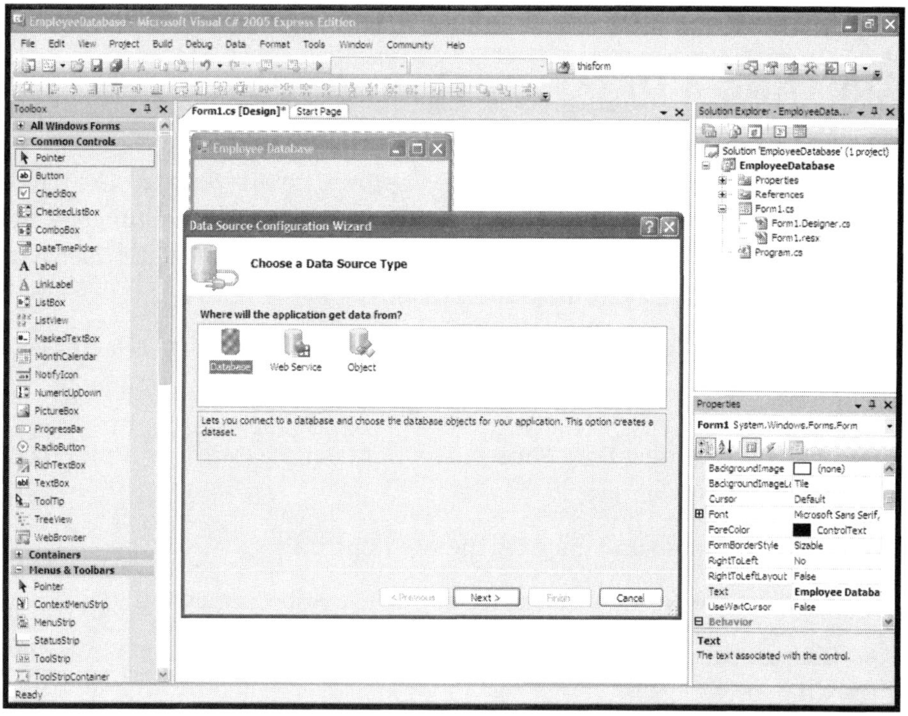

FIGURE 9-5

The Data Source Configuration Wizard.

We can also preview the data contained within a table:

1. Click on Data. The Data menu is displayed.

2. Click on Preview Data. The Preview Data dialog box is displayed.

3. Select the EmployeeDetails table and click on Preview. All the records contained within the EmployeeDetails table are displayed in the Results pane (see Figure 9-6).

4. Click on Close. The Preview Data dialog box closes.

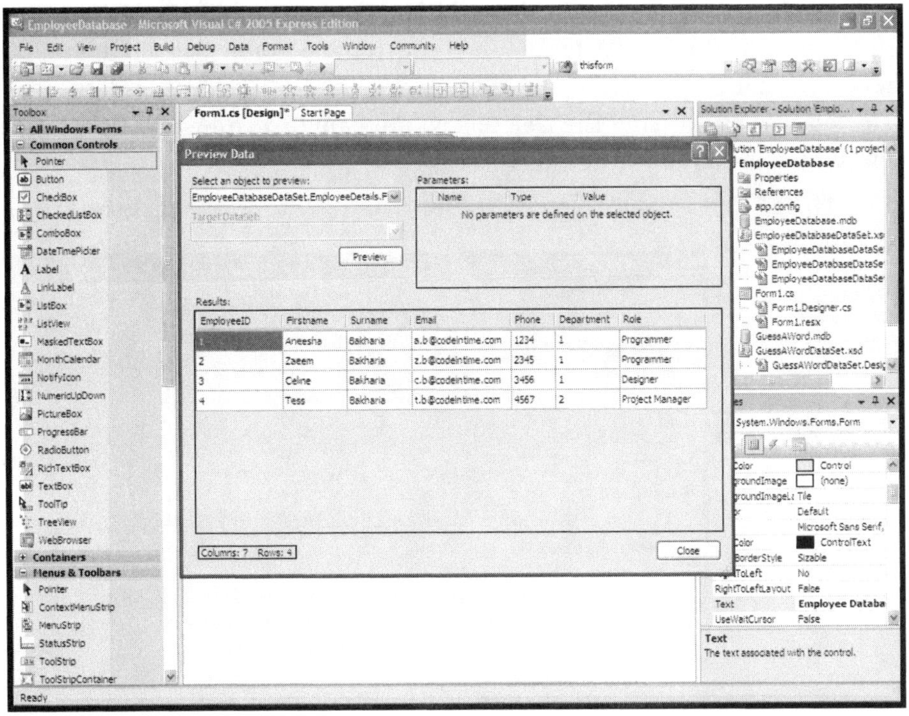

FIGURE 9-6

Previewing data retrieved from a database.

DISPLAYING DATA WITH THE DATAGRIDVIEW CONTROL

The DataGridView control displays on a form in an editable table the records retrieved from a database. The DataGridView control can be configured to display data as read only. In the example that follows, we will configure the DataGridView control to allow records to be edited, deleted, and added. Steps to add a DataGridView control are as follows:

1. Drag a DataGridView control onto a form. A DataGridView Task pane appears next to the control.

2. Click on the Dock with Parent Container link. The DataGridView control expands to fit the size of the form.

3. Select EmployeeDatabaseDataSet from the Data Source drop-down list.

4. Check the Enable Adding Records, Enable Editing Records, and Enable Deleting Records check boxes. These options allow data within the DataGridView control to be edited.

5. Press F5 to view the DataGridView control in action. The DataGridView control displays each record retrieved from the EmployeeDetails table.

Each record within the DataGridView control is editable (see Figure 9-7). We can edit each field. All changes we make are immediately saved back to the database. We can delete a selected row by pressing the Delete key. You can also enter additional records into the last row, which is marked with asterisks.

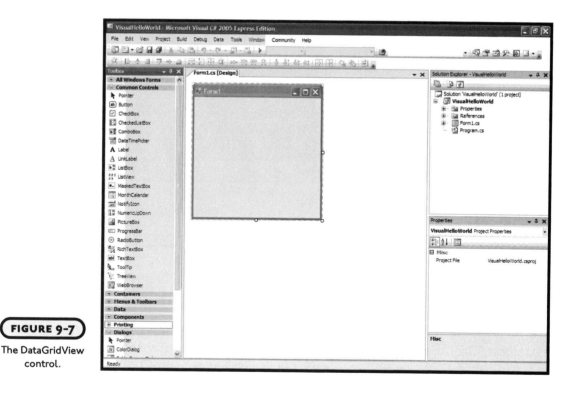

FIGURE 9-7

The DataGridView control.

DISPLAYING SEARCH RESULTS IN A DATAGRIDVIEW CONTROL

Typically, it is not practical to display all the records retrieved from a database within a DataGridView control. If there are many records, the user will have to manually scroll through the control and find the record. Ideally, we would like to provide a Search text entry box in which users can type what they are looking for, click on a button, and view the results in the DataGridView control. This is very easy to do in Visual C# 2005 Express Edition:

1. Drag a DataGridView control onto a form. A DataGridView Task pane appears next to the control.

2. Click on the Dock with Parent Container link. The DataGridView control expands to fit the size of the form.

3. Select employeeDatabaseDataSet from the Data Source drop-down list.

4. Check the Enable Adding Records, Enable Editing Records, and Enable Deleting Records check boxes. These options allow data within the DataGridView control to be edited.

5. Click on the Add Query link. The Search Criteria dialog box opens.

6. Enter the name of the query. Call the query Search for this example.

7. Add a WHERE clause to the query contained in the multiline query text field.

8. Add "Surname = ?" after the WHERE clause. This indicates that we want to search for a record by using criteria set in the Surname field. The ? tells Visual C# 2005 Express Edition that we want it to create a search interface for the specified criteria and place this interface above the DataGridView control.

9. Click on OK. The Search Criteria dialog box closes. A ToolBarStrip control is placed above the DataGridView control.

10. Press F5 to test the search. All records are initially displayed in the DataGridView control.

11. Enter a Surname and click on the Search button. Only search results that match the criteria (the surname you are searching for) are displayed (see Figure 9-8).

FIGURE 9-8

Searching for records with a DataGridView control.

We can, of course, still edit, delete, and add new records with the DataGridView control. As you can see from the preceding example, the DataGridView control is very versatile. When no search results are returned, a single blank row with an asterisk on its left is displayed. You can enter a new employee in this row.

BINDING DATA TO FORM CONTROLS

We now turn our attention to data binding. Data binding retrieves data from a database and displays this data in a custom-built form. We no longer need to be restricted to the grid or table-like display of the DataGridView control. The BindingSource control binds the data to the form controls. The BindingNavigator control adds a ToolStrip control to the form, with controls to navigate records. There are also buttons to delete records and add new records.

To display data retrieved from a database and display with a form control:

1. Create a new Windows Forms application called DataBindings.

2. Set the Text property of the default form to Employee Details.

3. Design the form shown in Figure 9-9. The form has TextBox and Label controls for each field in the EmployeeDetails table.

FIGURE 9-9

A simple form with data-bound controls.

4. Drag a BindingSource control onto the form. The control is added to the gray area beneath the form.

5. Set the Bindings property of the BindingSource control to EmployeeDatabaseDataset.

6. Set the DataMember property to EmployeeDetails.

7. Expand the DataBindings group of properties of each TextBox control and set the Tag property to the corresponding field within the BindingSource control. Set the Text property to the corresponding field within the BindingSource control as well.

8. Drag a BindingsNavigator control onto the form. A ToolStrip control with buttons to navigate through all of the records retrieved from the EmployeeDetails controls is displayed. Set the Bindings property to **employeeDetailsBindingSource**.

9. Press F5 to run the example. You can view individual records on a form, as well as navigate backward and forward through all returned records.

It really is this easy to display the data retrieved from a database within a form. In the next section, we will take a look at writing code in C# to retrieve data from a database.

Using C# Code to Retrieve Data from a Database

This section title is a little bit misleading because even though we've been using wizards and controls to retrieve and display data from a database, C# code has still been doing all the hard work. Visual C# Express 2005 has been doing a lot of intelligent work behind the scenes to create the required C#. This section shows you how you can write your own C# code to connect to, query, and display data retrieved from a database.

The first thing that we need to do is import the System.Data.OleDb namespace, which is required to connect to Microsoft Access databases. We would need to import System.Data.SQL if we were going to connect to a SQL Server database.

```
using System.Data.OleDb;
```

We then need to create a database connection, which we do with the OleDbConnection object. We need to provide the OleDbConnection object with a connection string that includes the path to the Access Database.

```
OleDbConnection conn = new OleDbConnection();
conn.ConnectionString = @"Provider=Microsoft.Jet.OLEDB.4.0;Data
Source=C:\Databases\GuessAWord.mdb";
conn.Open();
```

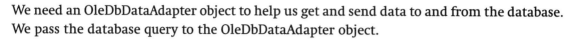

We need an OleDbDataAdapter object to help us get and send data to and from the database. We pass the database query to the OleDbDataAdapter object.

```
OleDbDataAdapter dataAdapter = new OleDbDataAdapter();
dAdapter = new OleDbDataAdapter("Select * from tbl_Words", conn);
```

We can store the data that is retrieved in a DataTable object, which is an in-memory table that contains all the records returned. The `Fill()` method of the DataAdapter object is used to copy the data into the DataTable object.

```
DataTable dtableWords = new DataTable();
dAdapter.Fill(dtableWords);
```

Each row of data can be accessed using a DataRow object. A column's value within a row can be retrieved and then assigned to a variable or a control's Text property. We would need to loop through all the rows to extract data for each record.

```
DataRow mRow = dtableWords.Rows[0];
GuessWord.Text=mRow["Word"].ToString();
```

The Count property of the DataTable object returns the number of records currently in the DataTable object:

```
dtableWords.Rows.Count;
```

Finally, we need to close the database connection:

```
conn.Close();
```

BACK TO THE GUESS A WORD GAME

To build the Guess A Word game, we need to complete the following tasks:

- Design a database to store the words and their associated clues.
- Design an interface that displays the clue and enables the user to enter the guessed word into a TextBox control.
- Write C# code to retrieve the words and their associated clues from the database.
- Check if the guess word is correct and inform the user.

DESIGNING THE DATABASE

We will create the database in Microsoft Access. We only need a single table, called tbl_Words (see Figure 9-10). Within this table, we need the following three fields:

- **WordID.** Stores our primary key and unique identifier.
- **Word.** Stores the words that the user must guess.
- **Clue.** Stores the clue.

Designing the Interface

The interface is very simple, as shown in Figure 9-11. We need the following controls:

- Label control to display the name of the game in a big and colorful font.
- Label control to display the clue.
- Textbox control for the user to enter the word.
- Button control that will trigger code to check if the guess word is correct and provide feedback.

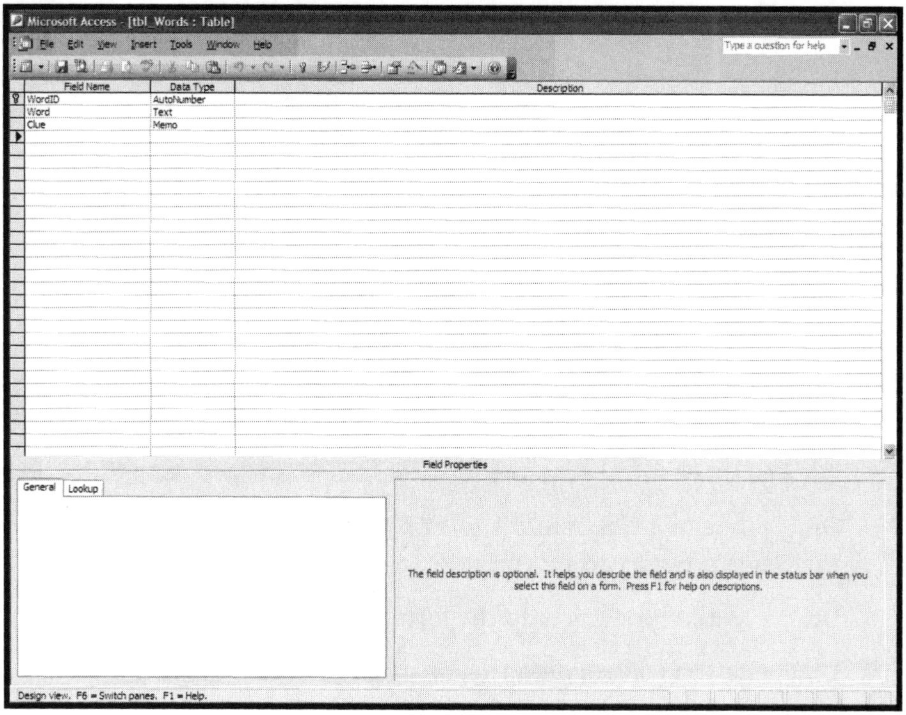

FIGURE 9-10

The tbl_Words table in the GuessAWord database.

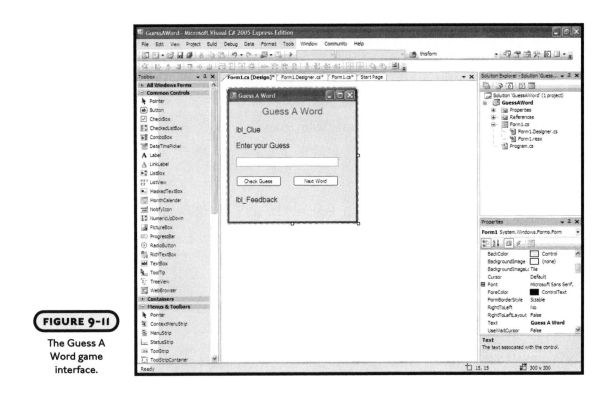

FIGURE 9-11

The Guess A
Word game
interface.

- Button control that will display the clue for the next word.
- Label control to provide feedback to the player.

Designing the Guess A Word interface:

1. Create a new Windows Forms application called GuessAWord.

2. Set the Text property of the default form to Guess A Word.

3. Drag a Label control onto the form. This will display the title of the game. Set the Text attribute to Guess A Word. Change the font, font size, and color properties.

4. Drag a Label control onto the form. Set the Name property to lbl_Clue.

5. Drag a Label control onto the form. Set the Text property to Enter your Guess:. Set the Name property to lbl_Instruction.

6. Drag a TextBox control onto the form. Set the Name property to tb_GuessedWord.

7. Drag a Button control onto the form. Set the Text property to Check Guess. Set the Name property to CheckGuess.

8. Drag a Button control onto the form. Set the Text property to Next Word. Set the Name property to NextWord. Set the Visible property to False.

9. Drag a Label control onto the form. Position the label below the Button control. Set the Name property to lbl_Feedback. Set the Visible property to False.

With the interface designed, we move on to writing the C# code in the next section.

Adding the C# Code

The code needs to retrieve the word and its clue. The word needs to be stored in a variable. The clue needs to be display by lbl_clue. When the button is clicked, the application needs to check if the text entered into tb_GuessedWord matches the word retrieved from the database.

1. Double-click on the Check Guess button. The Form1.cs file is displayed within the code panel.

2. Import the System.Data.OleDb namespace:

```
using System.Data.OleDb;
```

3. Add the following variables to the Form1 class:

```
OleDbConnection conn = new OleDbConnection();
OleDbDataAdapter dAdapter = new OleDbDataAdapter();
DataTable dtableWords = new DataTable();
int rowPos = 0;
int noWords = 0;
String currentWord = "";
```

4. Add the following code to the form's constructor method:

```
public Form1()
        {
                InitializeComponent();
                conn.ConnectionString =
@"Provider=Microsoft.Jet.OLEDB.4.0;Data Source=C:\Databases\GuessAWord.mdb";
                conn.Open();
                dAdapter = new OleDbDataAdapter("Select * from tbl_Words",
conn);
                dAdapter.Fill(dtableWords);
                DataRow mRow = dtableWords.Rows[rowPos];
```

```
        currentWord = mRow["Word"].ToString();
        currentWord = currentWord.ToLower();
        lbl_Clue.Text = "Clue: " + mRow["Clue"].ToString();
        noWords = dtableWords.Rows.Count;
    }
```

5. Add the following code to the **Check Guess** button's `onClick` handler:

```
private void CheckGuess_Click(object sender, EventArgs e)
    {
        lbl_Feedback.Visible = true;
        if (currentWord == tb_GuessedWord.Text.ToLower())
        {
            lbl_Feedback.Text = "Correct!";
            NextWord.Visible = true;
        }
        else
        {
            lbl_Feedback.Text = "Incorrect!";
        }
    }
```

6. Add the following code to the **Next Word** button's `onClick` handler:

```
        private void NextWord_Click(object sender, EventArgs e)
        {
            rowPos = rowPos + 1;
            if (rowPos < noWords)
            {
                DataRow mRow = dtableWords.Rows[rowPos];
                currentWord = mRow["Word"].ToString();
                currentWord = currentWord.ToLower();
                lbl_Clue.Text = "Clue: " + mRow["Clue"].ToString();
                noWords = dtableWords.Rows.Count;
                lbl_Feedback.Visible = false;
                NextWord.Visible = false;
                tb_GuessedWord.Text = "";
            }
            else
```

```
            {
                    lbl_Feedback.Visible = false;
                    CheckGuess.Visible = false;
                    NextWord.Visible = false;
                    tb_GuessedWord.Visible = false;
                    lbl_Instruction.Visible = false;
                    lbl_Clue.Text = "Game Completed!";
                    conn.Close();
            }
        }
```

The full code listing:

```
using System;
using System.Collections.Generic;
using System.ComponentModel;
using System.Data;
using System.Drawing;
using System.Text;
using System.Windows.Forms;
using System.Data.OleDb;

namespace GuessAWord
{
    public partial class Form1 : Form
    {
        OleDbConnection conn = new OleDbConnection();
        OleDbDataAdapter dAdapter = new OleDbDataAdapter();
        DataTable dtableWords = new DataTable();
        int rowPos = 0;
        int noWords = 0;
        String currentWord = "";

        public Form1()
        {
            InitializeComponent();
            conn.ConnectionString =
@"Provider=Microsoft.Jet.OLEDB.4.0;Data Source=C:\Databases\GuessAWord.mdb";
```

```csharp
                conn.Open();
                dAdapter = new OleDbDataAdapter("Select * from tbl_Words",
conn);

                dAdapter.Fill(dtableWords);
                DataRow mRow = dtableWords.Rows[rowPos];
                currentWord = mRow["Word"].ToString();
                currentWord = currentWord.ToLower();
                lbl_Clue.Text = "Clue: " + mRow["Clue"].ToString();
                noWords = dtableWords.Rows.Count;
            }

            private void CheckGuess_Click(object sender, EventArgs e)
            {
                lbl_Feedback.Visible = true;
                if (currentWord == tb_GuessedWord.Text.ToLower())
                {
                        lbl_Feedback.Text = "Correct!";
                        NextWord.Visible = true;
                }
                else
                {
                        lbl_Feedback.Text = "Incorrect!";
                }
            }

            private void NextWord_Click(object sender, EventArgs e)
            {
                rowPos = rowPos + 1;
                if (rowPos < noWords)
                {
                        DataRow mRow = dtableWords.Rows[rowPos];
                        currentWord = mRow["Word"].ToString();
                        currentWord = currentWord.ToLower();
                        lbl_Clue.Text = "Clue: " + mRow["Clue"].ToString();
                        noWords = dtableWords.Rows.Count;
                        lbl_Feedback.Visible = false;
                        NextWord.Visible = false;
```

```
                        tb_GuessedWord.Text = "";
                }
                else
                {
                        lbl_Feedback.Visible = false;
                        CheckGuess.Visible = false;
                        NextWord.Visible = false;
                        tb_GuessedWord.Visible = false;
                        lbl_Instruction.Visible = false;
                        lbl_Clue.Text = "Game Completed!";
                        conn.Close();
                }
        }
    }
}
```

Testing the Application

The following are some techniques to use to test the robustness of the game:

- Delete all the words in the database. How does the code deal with this? Should you add code to check whether no records exist in the database?

- Add new words of variable length to the database. Are you allowing enough character space in the Guess A Word TextBox control for the user to enter lengthy words?

- Are you able to display multiline clues in the Label control?

SUMMARY

We have covered a lot of new ground in this chapter. There is still much more to learn about databases. This chapter has only covered the basics. If you intend to use your C# skills to start building Web-based applications with ASP.NET, I encourage you to learn more about database design and access within the .NET Framework.

CHALLENGES

1. In Chapter 5, you developed a Word Finder Puzzle Generator. The words included in the Puzzle Generator were stored in an array within the program code. Enhance the Puzzle Generator so that the words are retrieved from a database.

2. Include categories within the Guess A Word game. You need to create a Categories table within the database and allow the player to select a category prior to being asked to guess the word.

3. Instead of providing textual clues in the Guess A Word game, display pictures. You need to alter the database to store a path to the image file. Use the PictureBox control to display the picture.

CHAPTER

ERROR HANDLING
AND DEBUGGING

Sometimes code refuses to compile, displays error messages while running, or just simply crashes. No matter how proficient or knowledgeable a programmer you are, you will always have to contend with errors. The ability to identify and fix errors is an important part of programming. Debugging code is both a time-consuming and rewarding task. As described in this chapter, Microsoft Visual C# 2005 Express Edition has numerous tools to help simplify the debugging process. We'll also be looking at generic debugging techniques. In this chapter you will learn how to:

- Differentiate between syntax, runtime, and logical errors.
- Use the debugging tools within Visual C# 2005 Express Edition.
- Set breakpoints in code.
- Monitor the contents of variables while debugging.
- Use the try and catch code block to gracefully handle runtime errors.
- Debug an existing Tic-Tac-Toe game.

PROJECT PREVIEW: THE TIC-TAC-TOE GAME

We won't be building a game in this chapter. Instead, we are going to fix the bugs in a Tic-Tac-Toe game. You've just been employed as a programmer and have been assigned to fix an existing game that is not working as expected. This is a very real-world scenario, because you won't always be building a project from scratch. Fixing and extending existing applications are essential tasks performed by programmers.

The Tic-Tac-Toe game (see Figure 10-1) has been coded in C# by a programmer who has since left the company. The game has no documentation and very few inline comments. The client has complained that the game has a bug, though no errors are displayed. The client has not provided a description of the bug, but requires a fixed version as soon as possible. Another programmer has attempted to fix the game, and now the C# code refuses to compile.

The Tic-Tac-Toe game is a two-player game. It has a simple interface comprised of clickable labels that can contain either X or O. Players take turns clicking on labels strategically to win the game by getting three X's or O's in either a horizontal, vertical, or diagonal row. In Figure 10-1, Player 2 has won by placing three O's in the middle horizontal row.

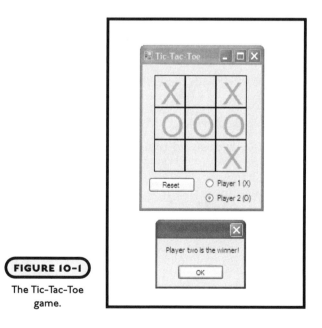

FIGURE 10-1

The Tic-Tac-Toe game.

TYPES OF ERRORS: SYNTAX, RUNTIME, AND LOGICAL

Syntax, runtime, and logical errors are three types of errors that you'll encounter. We took a brief look at syntax errors in Chapter 1. As your experience grows, identifying errors will become instinctive and routine. You'll also be able to take preemptive measures to stop errors from occurring.

Syntax errors are also known as compile-time or build errors. A syntax error prevents code from compiling. A syntax error occurs when incorrect C# language constructs are used. You'll encounter syntax errors while developing an application. Visual C# Express underlines syntax errors in red, as shown in Figure 10-2. This is great, because you don't have to wait to compile the code before you know that syntax errors exist.

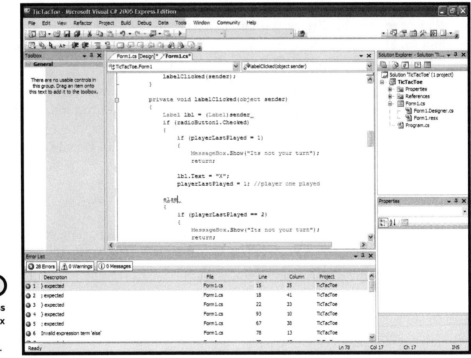

FIGURE 10-2

Visual C# Express underlines syntax errors in red as they are written.

Examples of syntax errors include the following:

- A missing semicolon at the end of a statement.
- Missing or misplaced braces, {}.
- A missing variable declaration.
- A misspelled variable or method name.
- Passing the incorrect number of parameters to a method.
- Passing variables with an incorrect type to a method.

A runtime error occurs after code has been executed and is running. Runtime errors throw exceptions and can be gracefully handled. A common example of a runtime error is code that tries to write to or read from a file that does not exist. It is important that you find runtime errors in testing and fix them before the application is distributed. The C# language has a try-catch exception-handling mechanism that we'll use to help make an application much more robust and display appropriate error messages to users. For example, using this mechanism before we distribute an application may help us to prevent a runtime error, by locating an attempt to read from a nonexistent file.

Logical errors, also known as semantic errors, sometimes can be elusive. A logical error occurs when a program does not work as intended; in other words, something is wrong with its internal logic. Logical errors are hard to fix and usually require a programmer to trace through code and look for errors. The debugging tools within Visual C# Express assist with locating logical errors.

DEBUGGING

Visual C# 2005 Express Edition has a special mode known as debug mode. When an application is compiled in debug mode, extra information is kept while the application runs. In debug mode, we can do the following:

- View the values stored in variables.
- Pause and restart application execution.
- Stop execution at a code statement.
- Step through code one line at a time.
- View changes to the contents of a variable as code is executed.

Compilation and execution information is written to the Output window. Figure 10-3 shows the contents of the Output window after successful compilation. The Output window is accessed from the Windows submenu within the Debug menu.

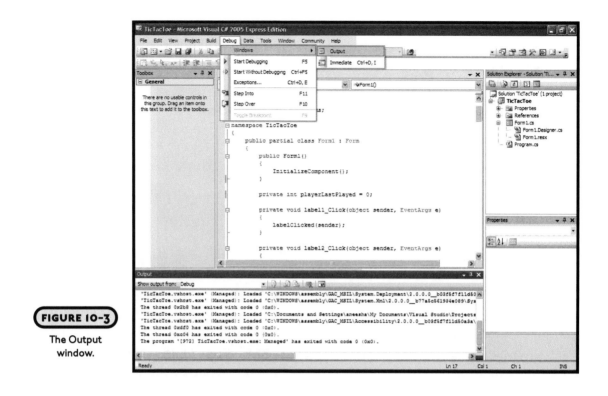

FIGURE 10-3

The Output window.

Adding Debug Statements to Code

The simplest technique to help debug an application involves printing the contents of a variable. This is usually accomplished by using the `Console.WriteLine()` method in a console application or displaying a debug statement on a Label control in a Windows Forms application. The problem is that we need to disable the debug code. This is achieved by preceding the code with `//`, which makes the code a comment. Comments are ignored by the compiler.

Here is a debug statement:

```
Console.WriteLine("Entering the for loop.");
```
Once our problem is fixed, we can either delete the debug code or make it a comment:
```
// Console.WriteLine("Entering the for loop.");
```
When we need to debug the code again, we simply remove `//` from the statement:
```
Console.WriteLine("Entering the for loop.");
```

Commenting and uncommenting code can be tedious and time consuming. Fortunately, a better way exists: using the `Debug.WriteLine()` method, located within the `System.Diagnostics` namespace. This method is executed only in debug mode. In normal or release mode, the `Debug.WriteLine()` method is ignored by the compiler.

The following is an example of using a `Debug.WriteLine()` statement:

```
Debug.WriteLine("Entering the for loop.");
```

This example shows how to print the contents of a variable, i, with a `Debug.WriteLine()` statement:

```
Debug.WriteLine("Loop Counter:" + i);
We can also group debug statements in categories:
Debug.WriteLine("Entering the for loop.","Category Name");
```

Setting a Breakpoint

The Debug toolbar, shown in Figure 10-4 in the upper-left corner, has a Pause button. The first four buttons manually control breaking. Once the Start or Play button is clicked, the other three buttons become enabled. Clicking the Pause button while an application is running enters break mode. This is not very useful, however, because application execution is very fast, and we can't accurately halt execution at a specific line of code by clicking a button. We need more fine-grained control over breaking for it to be a useful debugging technique. This is where a breakpoint comes in handy.

A breakpoint is a marker that we can place on a line of code, as shown in Figure 10-5. The breakpoint marker looks like a red ball. In debug mode, when this line is reached, execution is paused. There are two ways to add a breakpoint:

- Left-click on the gray area to the left of the line of code.
- Right-click on the code line and select Insert Breakpoint.

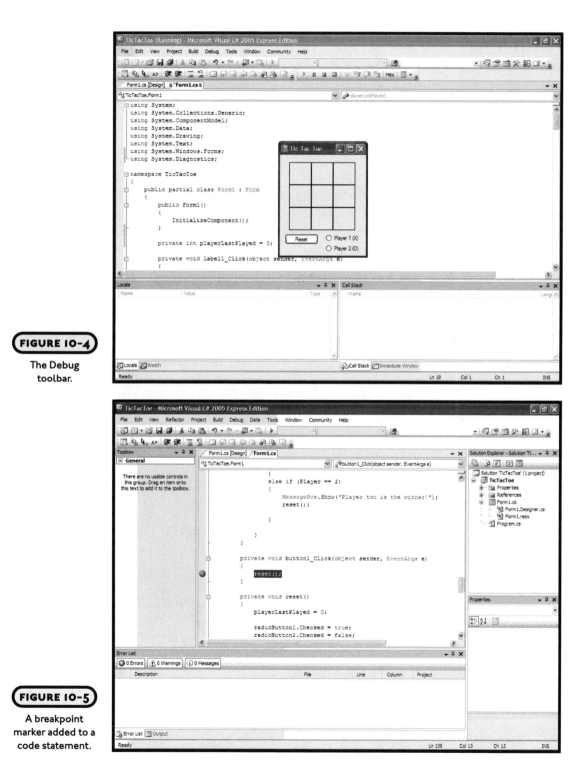

FIGURE 10-4

The Debug toolbar.

FIGURE 10-5

A breakpoint marker added to a code statement.

Monitoring Variables

When a program is paused in break mode, we can mouse over a variable in Code view and view its contents, which are displayed within a yellow tooltip, as depicted in Figure 10-6. This is very useful, because we can specify the exact location to stop code execution and view all the contents of variables at this time.

We can also view the result of an expression as a tooltip by highlighting it with the mouse, as illustrated in Figure 10-7.

You might have noticed that while running an application, the Solution Explorer window disappears. Two tabs, Locals and Watch, are displayed. These tabs provide additional and more complex ways to monitor variables as a program executes. Each tab lists the variables by name and includes their type and value.

The Locals tab, shown in Figure 10-8, lists all variables within the current scope.

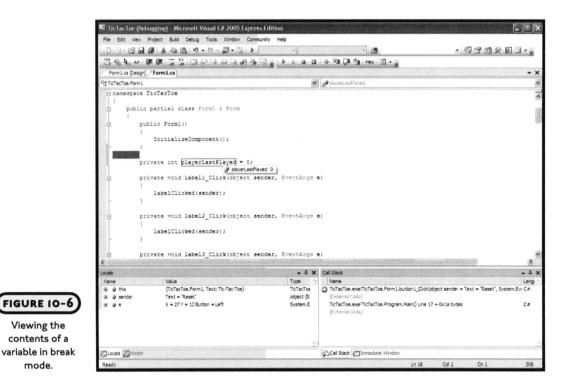

FIGURE 10-6

Viewing the contents of a variable in break mode.

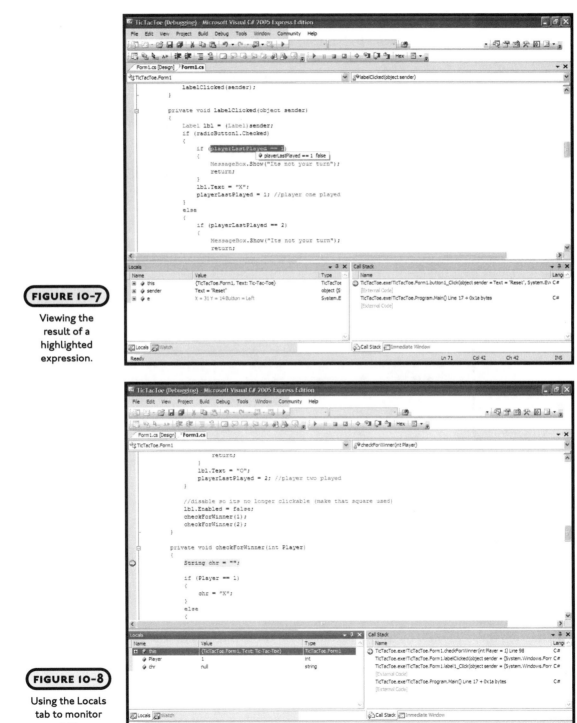

FIGURE 10-7

Viewing the
result of a
highlighted
expression.

FIGURE 10-8

Using the Locals
tab to monitor
variables.

In Figure 10-9, the Watch tab contains a customized list of variables that need to be monitored. You add additional variables by name to this list. One of the variables is an array. Complex variable types like arrays can be expanded to list their elements. Complex variables have a + symbol to their left that indicates that they can be expanded.

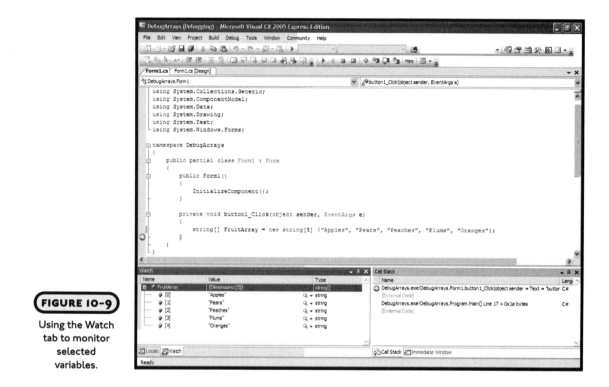

FIGURE 10-9

Using the Watch tab to monitor selected variables.

Stepping Through Code with the Debug Toolbar

While in break mode, we can view one line of code at a time. The idea is to run a line of code, check the contents of variables, and repeat this process until we can identify where a logical error is occurring. We can then fix the error and use the same technique to check that the logical error is fixed. An arrow is placed next to the line of code that is currently being executed.

We can step through code by using the following three buttons on the Debug toolbar:

- **Step Into.** Executes the current line and moves to the next line of code.
- **Step Over.** Does not execute nested code blocks.
- **Step Out.** Executes to the end of a code block and then resumes break mode at the statement that follows the code block.

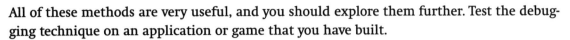

All of these methods are very useful, and you should explore them further. Test the debugging technique on an application or game that you have built.

Keyboard commands come in handy when stepping through code. Press F5 to continue code execution. F11 triggers the Step into button. F10 corresponds to clicking the Step over button. Shift+F11 is pressed to Step out of a code block.

STRUCTURED ERROR HANDLING

Exceptions are errors that are generated at runtime and display unfriendly and cryptic error messages to a user. C# allows us to detect such errors in a graceful and structured manner. Let's take a look at a common exception that occurs when we try to access an array element that does not exist:

```
int[] myArray;
myArray = new int[3] { 0, 1, 2 };
int myElement = myArray[4];
```

The `System.IndexOutOfRangeException` unhandled exception that the preceding code generates is displayed in Figure 10-10. This exception occurs when we try to access an element in an array that does not exist. The array, `myArray`, is declared to hold four elements. We can't access the third element with an index of 2, because element indexing begins at 0. So the third element is referenced like this:

```
int[] myArray;
myArray = new int[3] { 0, 1, 2 };
int myElement = myArray[3];
```

We use `try` and `catch` code blocks to handle an exception. Code that could potentially cause an exception is placed within a `try` block. A `catch` code block follows a `try` block and contains the code that must be executed if an exception occurs:

```
try
{
    // place code that must cause an exception within a try block
}
catch(Exception e)
{
    // place code that must be executed when an exception occurs
}
```

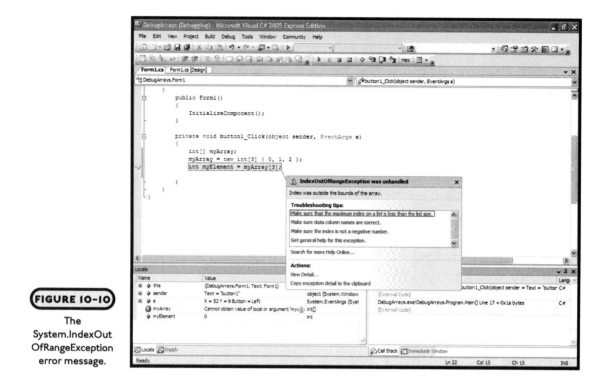

FIGURE 10-10

The
System.IndexOut
OfRangeException
error message.

The `catch` statements take an Exception type as a parameter. This is how you specify the type of exception that the catch block is programmed to handle. The generic Exception type catches all exceptions, including the `System.IndexOutOfRangeException`.

There is also an optional final code block, which contains code that must be executed after the `try` block or `catch` block:

```
try
{
    // place code that must cause an exception within a try block
}
catch(Exception e)
{
    // place code that must be executed when an exception occurs
}
finally
```

```
{
    // place code that must be executed even if no exception is thrown
}
```

Handling Specific Exceptions

We can also use a catch statement to handle both specific and generic exceptions. This allows us to generate appropriate error messages. Table 10-1 contains common exception classes. This is how we would catch a System.IndexOutOfRangeException with a catch block:

```
try
{
    int[] myArray;
    myArray = new int[3] { 0, 1, 2 };
    int myElement = myArray[4];
}
catch(IndexOutOfRangeException e)
{
    // place code that must be executed when an IndexOutOfRangeException occurs
}
catch(Exception e)
{
    // place code that must be executed when all other exceptions occurs
}
Here is example that catches a DivideByZeroException:
try
{
    int div = 10/0;
}
catch(DivideByZeroException e)
{
    // place code that must be executed when a DivideByZeroException occurs
}
catch(Exception e)
{
    // place code that must be executed when all other exceptions occurs
}
```

TABLE 9-1 C# EXCEPTION CLASSES

Exception	Type of Exception
System.DivideByZeroException	An attempt to divide by zero has been made.
System.ArithmaticException	An invalid mathematical operation has been performed.
System.IndexOutOfRangeException	An array element has been incorrectly indexed.
System.NullReferenceException	Object pointers are not initialized.
System.IO.IOException	Input/output operations, such as reading or writing to a file, have failed.

Ordering Multiple Exceptions

Multiple catch statements can be used to handle all possible combinations of exceptions that can occur. The catch block that contains a matching exception will only be executed. The order in which catch blocks are placed is important, because catch blocks are matched sequentially. The Exception type is a superclass of both the IndexOutOfRangeException and DivideByZeroException classes, and it must therefore be placed last.

The following code illustrates how multiple exceptions are ordered:

```
try
{
     int[] myArray;
     myArray = new int[3] { 0, 1, 2 };
     int myElement = myArray[4]/myArray[0];
}
catch(IndexOutOfRangeException e)
{
     // place code that must be executed when an IndexOutOfRangeException occurs
}
catch(DivideByZeroException e)
{
```

```
        // place code that must be executed when a DivideByZeroException occurs
}
catch(Exception e)
{
        // place code that must be executed when all other exceptions occurs
}
```

BACK TO THE TIC-TAC-TOE GAME

With an understanding of common debugging and exception-handling techniques, we return to fix the Tic-Tac-Toe game, which is a two-player game. Player 1 needs to place three X's in a horizontal, vertical, or diagonal row. Player 2, on the other hand, needs to get three O's in a horizontal, vertical, or diagonal row. The program makes sure that each player gets a turn in alternating fashion and announces the winner.

All that you have been told is that the game has a bug, but no error messages are displayed. Another programmer has tried to fix the bug, and the code no longer compiles. This means that you have to fix syntax errors before you can find the logical error. Assume that the bug is a logical error, not a runtime error, because a runtime error would produce an error message. The code is not documented, so at the very least you should make some attempt to include comments.

Understanding the Interface

Figure 10-11 shows the Tic-Tac-Toe game interface. The interface looks very simple. Each row of the game board contains three labels. Radio buttons are used to specify whether it's Player 1's or Player 2's turn. There is also a Reset button to start a new game.

You can use the Properties window to look up the properties of each form control that is included within the interface (see Figure 10-12). The first label in the top row is called label1, the second label in the top row is called label2, and the third label is called label3. This naming convention is used across all rows. The two radio buttons are called radioButton1 and radioButton2, respectively. The Reset button is called button1. Each label has an `onClick` handler.

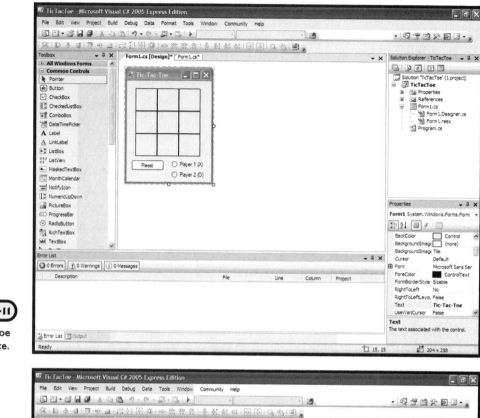

FIGURE 10-11

The Tic-Tac-Toe
game interface.

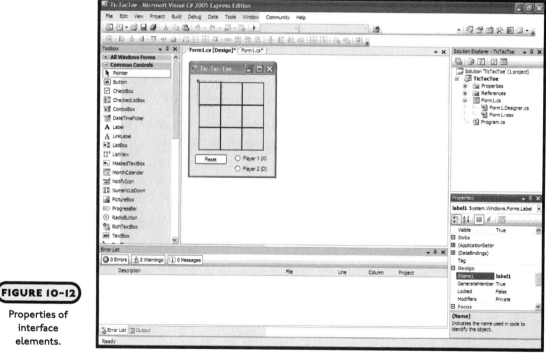

FIGURE 10-12

Properties of
interface
elements.

Understanding the C# Code

The `Form1.cs` file contains the code. A quick glance reveals the following three key methods:

- `labelClicked()`. Places either an X or an O on the label, depending upon which player's turn it is, and then checks if there is a winner.
- `CheckForWinner(int Player)`. Checks if the player that matches the number passed to it has won the game. This method contains a rather complex if statement that checks if three X's or O's are in a vertical, horizontal, or diagonal row. We have concluded that there is a logical error, so this method should be the first place we look.
- `Reset()`. Clears all labels and enables them so that they can be clicked on again.

Debugging the Game

The first thing we are going to do is find and fix the syntax error. We do this by trying to compile the game. The details of the syntax error are shown in Figure 10-13. Luckily, the syntax error seems pretty simple. It appears that a closing } is missing. Upon further investigation, we discover that the final } for the TicTacToe namespace has accidentally been deleted. Let's put it back and try to compile the code again.

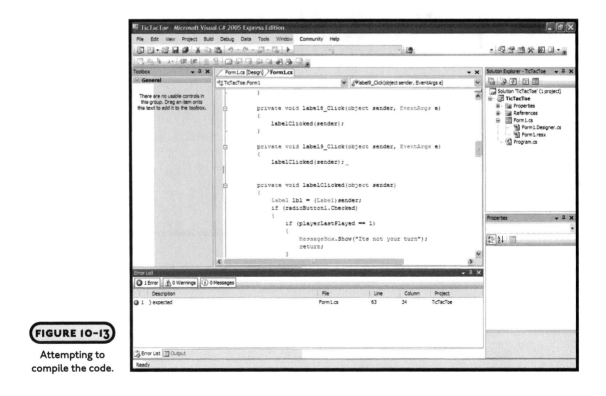

FIGURE 10-13

Attempting to compile the code.

It compiles, so we can now try to find that elusive bug. We inspect the CheckForWinner() method in more detail. We can't find any errors with the complex logic that checks for a winner. All the vertical, horizontal, and diagonal rows are checked. There aren't too many variables, so monitoring a variable won't be of much use. Where is that error? Any ideas?

Maybe we should check whether all the labels have been placed in the correct position and in the correct order. After inspecting the properties of each label, we discover that label8 is placed before label7 in the last row (see Figure 10-14). This means that a win in a diagonal row will never be detected. The fix is simple; we need to swap label8 and label7. This illustrates the importance of correctly naming and positioning form controls, because they too can contribute to difficult-to-debug errors. Mission accomplished!

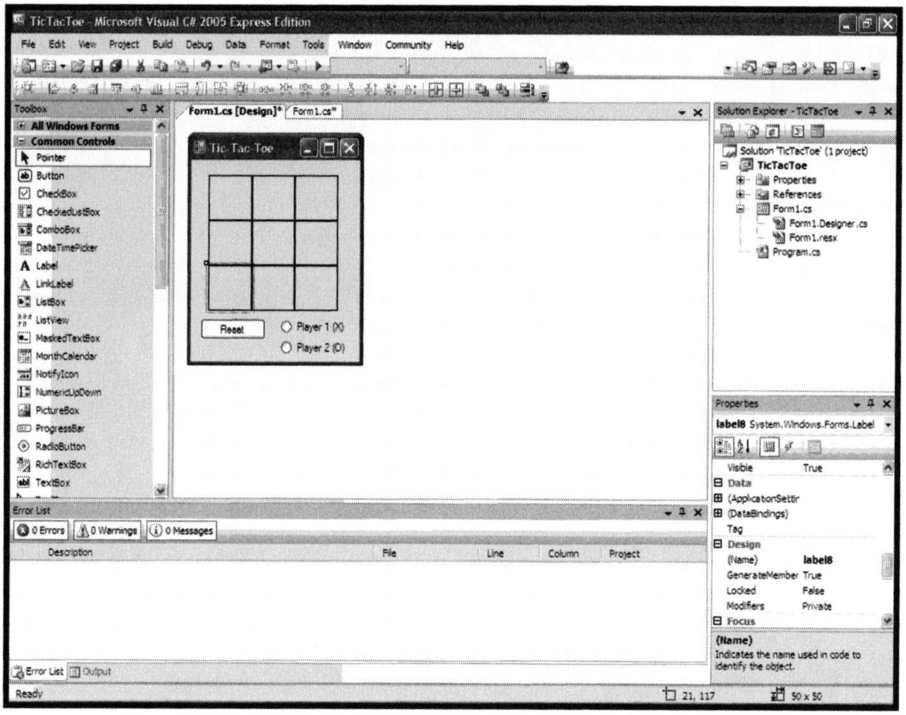

FIGURE 10-14

Mixed up labels in the Tic-Tac-Toe game.

The full code listing:

```
using System;
using System.Collections.Generic;
using System.ComponentModel;
using System.Data;
using System.Drawing;
using System.Text;
using System.Windows.Forms;

namespace TicTacToe
{
    public partial class Form1 : Form
    {
        public Form1()
        {
            InitializeComponent();
        }

        private int playerLastPlayed = 0;

        private void label1_Click(object sender, EventArgs e)
        {
            labelClicked(sender);
        }

        private void label2_Click(object sender, EventArgs e)
        {
            labelClicked(sender);
        }

        private void label3_Click(object sender, EventArgs e)
        {
            labelClicked(sender);
        }
```

```csharp
private void label4_Click(object sender, EventArgs e)
{
    labelClicked(sender);
}

private void label5_Click(object sender, EventArgs e)
{
    labelClicked(sender);
}

private void label6_Click(object sender, EventArgs e)
{
    labelClicked(sender);
}

private void label7_Click(object sender, EventArgs e)
{
    labelClicked(sender);
}

private void label8_Click(object sender, EventArgs e)
{
    labelClicked(sender);
}

private void label9_Click(object sender, EventArgs e)
{
    labelClicked(sender);
}

private void labelClicked(object sender)
{
    Label lbl = (Label)sender;
    if (radioButton1.Checked)
    {
        if (playerLastPlayed == 1)
```

```
        {
            MessageBox.Show("Its not your turn");
            return;
        }
        lbl.Text = "X";
        playerLastPlayed = 1; //player one played
    }
    else
    {
        if (playerLastPlayed == 2)
        {
            MessageBox.Show("Its not your turn");
             return;
        }
        lbl.Text = "O";
        playerLastPlayed = 2; //player two played
    }

    //disable so its no longer clickable (make that square used)
    lbl.Enabled = false;
    checkForWinner(1);
    checkForWinner(2);
}

private void checkForWinner(int Player)
{
    String chr = "";

    if (Player == 1)
    {
        chr = "X";
    }
    else
    {
        chr = "O";
    }
```

```
        if (((label1.Text == chr) && (label2.Text == chr) && (label3.Text == chr))
        || ((label4.Text == chr) && (label5.Text == chr) && (label6.Text == chr))
        || ((label7.Text == chr) && (label8.Text == chr) && (label9.Text == chr))
        || ((label1.Text == chr) && (label4.Text == chr) && (label7.Text == chr))
        || ((label2.Text == chr) && (label5.Text == chr) && (label8.Text == chr))
        || ((label3.Text == chr) && (label6.Text == chr) && (label9.Text == chr))
        || ((label1.Text == chr) && (label5.Text == chr) && (label9.Text == chr))
        || ((label3.Text == chr) && (label5.Text == chr) && (label7.Text == chr)))
        {

            //we found a winner
            if (Player == 1)
            {
                MessageBox.Show("Player one is the winner!");
                reset();
            }
            else if (Player == 2)
            {
                MessageBox.Show("Player two is the winner!");
                reset();

            }

        }
    }

    private void button1_Click(object sender, EventArgs e)
    {
        reset();
    }

    private void reset()
    {
        playerLastPlayed = 0;

        radioButton1.Checked = true;
        radioButton2.Checked = false;
```

```
            label1.Text = "";
            label1.Enabled = true;

            label2.Text = "";
            label2.Enabled = true;

            label3.Text = "";
            label3.Enabled = true;

            label4.Text = "";
            label4.Enabled = true;

            label5.Text = "";
            label5.Enabled = true;

            label6.Text = "";
            label6.Enabled = true;

            label7.Text = "";
            label7.Enabled = true;

            label8.Text = "";
            label8.Enabled = true;

            label9.Text = "";
            label9.Enabled = true;
        }
    }
}
```

SUMMARY

This has been a very important chapter. You have learned how to write resilient C# code that is able to gracefully handle exceptions. You have also learned generic debugging and problem-solving techniques that you can apply to all future applications and games that you will build. Always remember that a good programmer not only knows how to write code, but also is good at finding and fixing elusive bugs.

CHALLENGES

1. Write a program that divides two numbers provided by the user and gracefully handles a division by zero exception. You will need to design a Windows Forms interface.

2. Identify five common syntax errors.

3. Identify five common exceptions and explain how these exceptions can be handled gracefully.

4. Enhance the Tic-Tac-Toe game by including a virtual opponent (i.e., let the computer be Player 2).

READING AND WRITING FILES

T he ability to store and retrieve data is a trivial yet important part of programming. As computer users, we take for granted the mechanics of saving a CV as a Microsoft Word document and sending it to a potential employee. As a programmer, however, saving files is standard functionality that we need to incorporate in the games and applications that we build. In this chapter, we focus on the important classes within the System.IO namespace that allow us to check file properties as well as store and retrieve data. In this chapter you'll learn how to:

- Display information about files and folders.
- Read data from a text file.
- Write data to a text file.
- Append data to a text file.
- Copy, move, and delete files.
- Create, move, and delete folders.
- Use the File Open and File Save As dialog boxes.
- List the contents of a folder.
- Create a Rich Text Editor.

PROJECT PREVIEW: THE RICH TEXT EDITOR

Microsoft Word is a popular word processor that I am sure you have had the pleasure of using. Common features of a word processor include the ability to author, edit, and format a document. Microsoft Word certainly has a very impressive list of formatting options, as shown in Figure 11-1. Learning how to program the capability to select and format text intrigues many beginner programmers. In this chapter, I hope to take the mystery out of building a simple word processor. This project fits well with the overall theme of this chapter—storing and retrieving data. This chapter focuses primarily on saving text files, so our challenge within this project will be to save our formatted text to Rich Text Format (RTF).

The application we are going to build is called "Rich Text Editor" and is shown in Figure 11-2. We are also going to build a Simple Text Editor that is similar to Notepad, but I'm sure you'll be more excited about building the Rich Text Editor. The Rich Text Editor application will be a Windows Forms application.

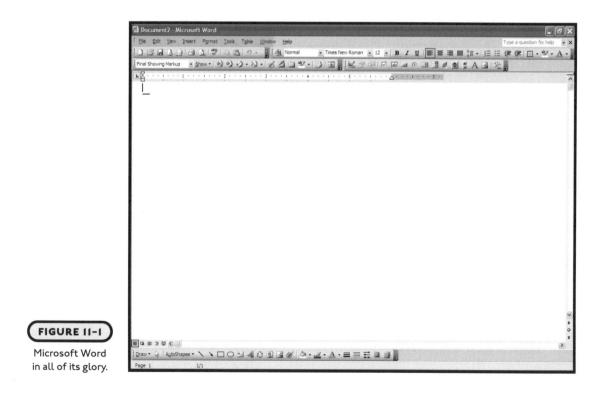

FIGURE 11-1

Microsoft Word
in all of its glory.

Notice in Figure 11-2 that the Rich Text Editor has a toolbar with buttons for some common formatting options, Bold, Italic, and Underline. This is not quite as impressive as the toolbars used in Microsoft Word, but it is still highly relevant and achievable for a beginner.

The Rich Text Editor, like Microsoft Word, is a What You See Is What You Get (WYSIWYG) application. This means that as a user formats the text, he sees what the formatting of the document looks like in real time. Figure 11-2 shows several lines of a document that have been formatted in different ways by a user. You may be thinking that this functionality is very complex and will take a lot of C# code to implement. However, while this may seem complex, the built-in tools and controls within Visual C# Express 2005 make it very straightforward. By the end of this chapter, you will appreciate the productivity enhancements within Visual C# Express 2005.

The Rich Text Editor will also use dialog boxes to help the user open and save documents. In Figure 11-3, a user is saving the currently formatted document, Sample.rtf, to a new folder on his hard drive (C drive) called RichTextEditorFiles. This chapter covers the OpenFileDialog and SaveFileDialog controls, which we'll use in this project to create the dialog boxes.

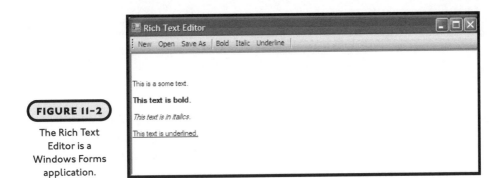

FIGURE 11-2

The Rich Text Editor is a Windows Forms application.

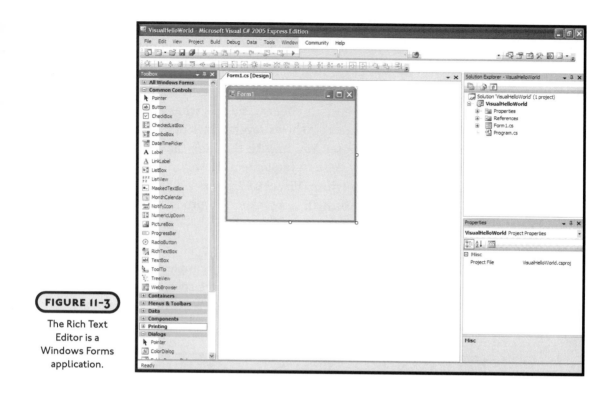

FIGURE II-3

The Rich Text
Editor is a
Windows Forms
application.

THE SYSTEM.IO NAMESPACE

The System.IO namespace contains classes and methods that relate to the Windows file system. The functionality for everything from creating files to listing the contents of a folder is found in a class within the System.IO namespace. In this chapter, we'll be using classes found in this namespace extensively.

The following line of code is used to import the System.IO namespace, and it is placed at the top of your C# code:

```
Using System.IO;
```

The System.IO namespace contains both static and instance classes. In a static class, you are able to use the methods within the class without first creating an object, which makes sense in situations where you need to use only a single method, such as to check whether a file exists. The File, Directory, and Path classes are static. In the example that follows, we use the Exists() method of the File class. The Exists() method returns a True value if the file is found.

```
File.Exists(@"C:/filename.txt");
```

In instance classes, such as FileInfo and DirectoryInfo, you have to create an object instance before you are able to call any of the methods contained within these classes. Here is an example of using the FileInfo class to check whether a file exists:

```
FileInfo file = new FileInfo(@"C:/filename.txt");
File.Exists;
```

DISPLAYING FILE AND FOLDER INFORMATION

The FileInfo class contains properties to determine whether a file exits, the size of a file in bytes, and the extension of a file, such a .txt or .doc. The FileInfo class is an instance class, so we have to first create a FileInfo object and then call the properties. In the next example, we import the System.IO namespace, check if a file exists, write file properties such as DirectoryName, Extension, Length, and Name to the console:

```
string txtFilePath = "C:\\sample.txt";
FileInfo file = new FileInfo(txtFilePath);
if (file.Exists)
{
        Console.WriteLine(Directoryfile.Directory.ToString());
        Console.WriteLine(file.DirectoryName.ToString());
        Console.WriteLine(file.Extension.ToString());
        Console.WriteLine(file.Length.ToString());
        Console.WriteLine(file.Name.ToString());
}
else
{
        Console.WriteLine("The file does not exist.");
}
```

READING A FILE

I think you'll be pleasantly surprised to find out how easy it is to retrieve text from a file. The ReadLine() method within the StreamReader class retrieves a line of text within the file, each time it is called. Reading text from a file is summarized in the following steps:

1. Import the System.IO namespace.

2. Create a StreamReader object by calling the File.OpenText() method.

3. Call the ReadLine() method to retrieve the first line from the file.

4. Use a while loop to continue to retrieve lines of text (by calling the `ReadLine()` method).

5. Exit the while loop when `ReadLine()` is null. ReadLine returns null when the end of the file is reached.

6. Close the StreamReader object.

In this example, the file is printed line by line to the console:

```
string fileLine;
StreamReader fileSR = File.OpenText("C:\\ReadFileSample.txt");
fileLine=fileSR.ReadLine();
while(fileLine!=null)
{
        Console.WriteLine(fileLine);
        fileLine=fileSR.ReadLine();
}
fileSR.Close();
```

Storing Data in a File

We are not restricted to reading data; we can also write data to a file. We need to use the StreamWriter class instead of the StreamReader class, which is used only for reading text files. The `WriteLine()` method within the StreamWriter class writes a line of text to a file. Writing text to a file is summarized in the following steps:

1. Import the System.IO namespace.

2. Create a StreamWriter object by calling the `File.CreateText()` method.

3. Write each line of text to a file using the `WriteLine()` file.

4. Close the StreamWriter object.

Let's use these steps to create a text file with a few lines of text:

```
StreamWriter fileSW = File.CreateText("C:\\WriteFileSample.txt");
fileSW.WriteLine("This is the first Line");
fileSW.WriteLine("This is second line");
fileSW.Close();
```

APPENDING DATA TO A FILE

We can also add data at the end of a file—known as *appending* data to a file. The WriteLine() method within the StreamWriter class is used to add lines of text to the file. Appending text to a file is summarized in the following steps:

1. Import the System.IO namespace.

2. Create a StreamWriter object by calling the File.AppendText() method.

3. Add each line of text to a file using the WriteLine() file.

4. Close the StreamWriter object.

We can now add text to the file that we created in the previous section:

```
StreamWriter fileSW = File.AppendText("C:\\WriteFileSample.txt");
fileSW.WriteLine("Appended Line 1");
fileSW.WriteLine("Appended Line 2");
fileSW.Close();
```

USING DIALOG BOXES TO CREATE A SIMPLE TEXT EDITOR

Thus far, you have learned how to read the contents of a text file, as well as create and save data to a new file. All of our code examples have been console applications. We are now going to use the File, StreamWriter, and StreamReader classes within a Windows Forms application. The application, called Simple Text Editor, is very similar to Notepad. Users will be able to create new files, open and edit existing files, and save files.

Dialog boxes are an essential element in migrating our console-based code examples to a visual and intuitive application. In our console application code snippets, the paths to the files that we were saving or reading from were hard-coded. Dialog boxes allow the user to browse the file system and specify the location and name of a file to open or save. The Simple Text Editor needs to include File Open and Save As dialog boxes.

Designing the Interface

Our interface, shown in Figure 11-4, resembles Notepad. We have a File menu that has three menu items: New, Open, and Save As. There is also a multiline TextBox control. Text that is retrieved from a file is displayed within this TextBox control, where a user can edit it. Text for a new file is also entered into this TextBox control. Follow these steps to create this application in Visual C# 2005 Express Edition:

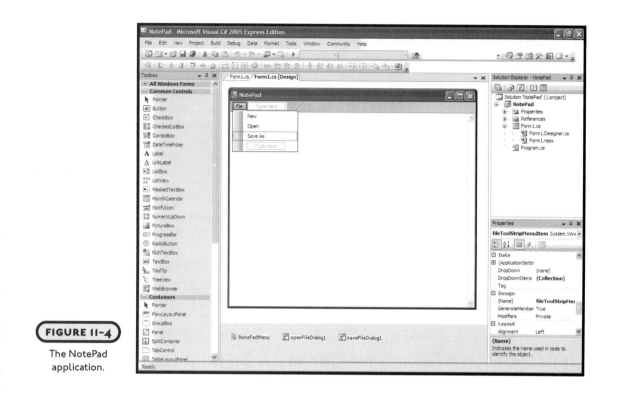

FIGURE 11-4

The NotePad
application.

1. Create a new Windows Forms application called NotePad.

2. Set the Text property of the form to NotePad.

3. Drag a MenuStrip control onto the form. The control will be added to the pane at the bottom of the forms designer.

4. Change the Name property of the MenuStrip control to NotePadMenu.

5. At the top of the form, you'll see the text Type Here. Click on this text and type File followed by pressing the Enter key. This creates the File menu.

6. Another Type Here text message is displayed below the File menu. Click on this text and type New; then press Enter. The New menu item is created.

7. Another Type Here text message is displayed below the New menu item. Click on this text and type Open; then press Enter. The Open menu item is created.

8. Another Type Here text message is displayed below the Open menu item. Click on this text and type Save As; then press Enter. The Save As menu item is created.

9. Drag a TextBox control onto the form. Set the Name property to textBoxEdit. Set the Multiline property to True. Set the Scrollbars property to Both.

10. We still need to make the multiline TextBox control fill the form. To do this, set the Dock property to Fill (i.e., select the middle square).

11. Double-click on the New menu item. The Form1.cs tab will be displayed within the code editor. A newToolStripMenuItem_Click() method will be created automatically. This method needs to set the filename variable to "Untitled" and clear the textBoxEdit control. The filename variable needs to be accessed by other methods, so we are going to make it a class level variable.

```
private void newToolStripMenuItem_Click(object sender, EventArgs e)
{
        filename = "Untitled";
        textBoxEdit.Clear();
        SetFormTitle();
}
```

12. Declare and initialize the filename variable as a string. Place this code at the beginning of the class file.

```
private string filename = "Untitled";
```

13. Each time a file is opened, a new file is created, or an existing file is saved with a new name, the title of the Simple Text Editor form needs to change. Having a centralized method to perform this task will reduce code replication. The SetFormTitle() method will perform this task by using the FileInfo class to retrieve and display the name of a file.

```
protected void SetFormTitle()
{
        FileInfo fileinfo = new FileInfo(filename);
        this.Text = fileinfo.Name + " - NotePad";
}
```

14. Click on the Form1.cs[Design] tab. The Simple Text Editor form is displayed.

The Open File Dialog Box

It's time to turn our attention to the OpenFileDialog control. The OpenFileDialog control will allow the user to navigate through drives and folders and select the text file (*.txt) that they want to open and display within the multiline TextBox control for editing. The OpenFileDialog box is dragged onto the form from the toolbox. Dialog boxes are not added to the current form; rather, they are added to the pane at the bottom of the Windows Forms Design View. The OpenFileDialog control can then be displayed from within C# code by calling its ShowDialog() method. If a user has clicked on the OK button, the DialogResult.OK result is returned, and the selected file is stored in the FileName property of the OpenFileDialog control.

Let's add a OpenFileDialog box to our Simple Text Editor:

1. Drag an OpenFileDialog control onto the form.

2. Double-click on the Open menu item. The Form1.cs file will be displayed within the code editor. An openToolStripMenuItem_Click() method will be created automatically. The openToolStripMenuItem_Click() method needs to contain the following code, which uses a StreamReader object to read the text from the specified file and display the text within the textBoxEdit control:

```
private void openToolStripMenuItem_Click(object sender, EventArgs e)
{
        if (openFileDialog1.ShowDialog() == DialogResult.OK)
        {
                filename = openFileDialog1.FileName;
                SetFormTitle();
        }
        using (StreamReader reader = File.OpenText(filename))
        {
                textBoxEdit.Clear();
                textBoxEdit.Text = reader.ReadToEnd();
        }
}
```

The Save Dialog Box

The SaveFileDialog control functions just like the OpenFileDialog control. It also allows the user to choose where a file must be saved and specify a file name. When a SaveFileDialog control is added to the form, it is displayed on the pane at the bottom of the Forms designer.

The ShowDialog() method is used to display the dialog box, and DialogResult.OK is returned if the user has entered a file name and location. The FileName property contains the file name, as specified by the user. Now, to add the remaining functionality that saves our edited text files, follow these steps:

1. Drag a SaveFileDialog control onto the form.

2. Double-click on the Open menu item. The Form1.cs file will be displayed within the code editor. A saveToolStripMenuItem_Click() method has also been created automatically. The saveToolStripMenuItem_Click() method needs to contain the following code, which uses a StreamWriter object to retrieve the text from the textBoxEdit control and save it to the specified file:

```
private void saveToolStripMenuItem_Click(object sender, EventArgs e)
{
        if (saveFileDialog1.ShowDialog() == DialogResult.OK)
        {
                filename = saveFileDialog1.FileName;
        }
        Stream stream = File.OpenWrite(filename);
        using (StreamWriter writer = new StreamWriter(stream))
        {
                writer.Write(textBoxEdit.Text);
        }
}
```

The Simple Text Editor is ready to be tested. Test all of its functionality by creating new text files, as well as opening and saving existing files.

The full code listing for the NotePad application:

```
using System;
using System.Collections.Generic;
using System.ComponentModel;
using System.Data;
using System.Drawing;
using System.Text;
using System.Windows.Forms;
using System.IO;


namespace NotePad
```

```csharp
{

    public partial class Form1 : Form
    {
        private string filename = "Untitled";

        public Form1()
        {
            InitializeComponent();
        }

        private void newToolStripMenuItem_Click(object sender, EventArgs e)
        {
            filename = "Untitled";
            textBoxEdit.Clear();
            SetFormTitle();
        }

        private void openToolStripMenuItem_Click(object sender, EventArgs e)
        {
            if (openFileDialog1.ShowDialog() == DialogResult.OK)
            {
                filename = openFileDialog1.FileName;
                SetFormTitle();
            }
            using (StreamReader reader = File.OpenText(filename))
            {
                textBoxEdit.Clear();
                textBoxEdit.Text = reader.ReadToEnd();
            }
        }

        private void saveToolStripMenuItem_Click(object sender, EventArgs e)
        {
            if (saveFileDialog1.ShowDialog() == DialogResult.OK)
            {
                filename = saveFileDialog1.FileName;
            }
            Stream stream = File.OpenWrite(filename);
```

```
        using (StreamWriter writer = new StreamWriter(stream))
        {
            writer.Write(textBoxEdit.Text);
        }
    }
    protected void SetFormTitle()
    {
        FileInfo fileinfo = new FileInfo(filename);
        this.Text = fileinfo.Name + " - NotePad";
    }
}
}
```

COPYING, MOVING, AND DELETING FILES

After a file is created, we can make a copy of it and place the copy in a new location, move the file to a new location, or delete the file if it is no longer needed. The File class has Copy(), Move(), and Delete() methods. The File class is a static class, so we don't need to create an object instance before we are able to use its methods.

The Copy() method takes two parameters. The first parameter is the file location of the file to be copied. The second parameter is the path location and file name of the copied file. After the Copy() method has been run, a file will exist in both locations. This is a very simple example that copies a file to a new location:

```
// Copy a File
Console.WriteLine("Copying File...");
File.Copy("C:\\csharpbook\\sample.txt","C:\\csharpbook\\samplecopy.txt");
Console.WriteLine("Done");
```

The Move() method works much like the Copy() method. It also takes two parameters. The first parameter is the location of the file to be moved. The second parameter is the location to where the file must be moved. This is a very simple example that moves a file to a new location:

```
// Move a File
Console.WriteLine("Moving File...");
File.Move("C:\\csharpbook\\samplecopy.txt","C:\\csharpbook\\flowcharts\\samplecopy.tx
t");
Console.WriteLine("Done");
```

The Delete() method simply deletes a file. The Delete() method takes only one parameter, the location of the file that must be deleted. The following is an example:

```
// Delete a File
Console.WriteLine("Deleting File...");
File.Delete("C:\\csharpbook\\sample2.txt");
Console.WriteLine("Done") ;
```

CREATING, MOVING, AND DELETING FOLDERS

The Directory class is also a static class. The Directory class contains methods that are useful for reorganizing a file system. It has methods to create folders, move folders, and delete folders.

The CreateDirectory() method, as its name suggests, creates a new directory. The method takes a single parameter, which is used to specify the path and name of the folder:

```
// Create a Directory
Console.WriteLine("Creating a Directory...");
Directory.CreateDirectory("C:\\csharpbook\\newdir");
```

The Move() method moves a folder and its contents to another location. The method takes two parameters. The first parameter specifies the current path and the name of the folder. The second parameter specifies the new location of the folder:

```
// Move a Directory
Console.WriteLine("Moving a Directory...");
Directory.Move("C:\\csharpbook\\newdir","C:\\csharpbook\\flowcharts\\newdir");
```

The Move() method does not work across drive volumes. This means that you can't move C:\ to D:\.

The Delete() folder method deletes a folder and all of the files and folders contained within that folder. The Delete() method takes only one parameter, which is the path to the folder that must be deleted.

```
// Delete a Directory
Console.WriteLine("Deleting a Directory...");
Directory.Delete("C:\\csharpbook\\flowcharts\\newdir");
```

LISTING DIRECTORIES

A folder usually contains subfolders and files. The GetFiles() method returns all of the files found at the root level of the folder. The GetDirectories() method lists all of the folders contained within a specified folder at the root level. Both of these methods are used to display the contents of a directory.

Let's list all the files found at a root level in the folder:

```
string directoryPath = "c:\\net_files";
string[] files = Directory.GetFiles(directoryPath);
for(int i=0;i< files.Length;i++)
{
        Console.WriteLine(files[i]);
}
```

Listing the directories within a folder at the root level is just as simple:

```
string[] subDirectories = Directory.GetDirectories(directoryPath);
for(int i=0;i< subDirectories.Length;i++)
{
        Console.WriteLine(subDirectories[i]);
}
```

LISTING DRIVES

A computer usually has many disk drives attached. The GetLogicalDrives() method within the Directory class returns all of the disk drives that are found on the computer where this code is running. The following example lists all of the drives attached to your computer:

```
foreach (string drive in Directory.GetLogicalDrives())
{
        Console.WriteLine(drive);
}
```

BACK TO THE RICH TEXT EDITOR APPLICATION

Equipped with our knowledge of dialog boxes and the StreamReader and StreamWriter classes, we are now ready to tackle the Rich Text Editor project. I'm sure there are still many things that you are unsure about and don't know how to program in C# or Visual C# 2005 Express Edition, including the following:

- Saving formatted text in RTF format.
- Retrieving formatted text from an RTF file.
- Displaying formatted text on a form.

- Allowing formatted text to be edited on a form.
- Allowing the user to select text within a document and apply formatting such as bold and italic.

How are we going build all of this? The answer is simple. We don't need to build a new control because we can use an existing one. Visual C# 2005 Express Edition includes a RichTextBox control. This RichTextBox control includes all of the functionality that we require—all we need to do is add it to a form and design the interface. Table 11-1 contains all the events associated with the RichTextBox control. Table 11-2 displays the important methods we'll be using to build this project.

TABLE 11-1 EVENTS TRIGGERED BY THE RICHTEXTBOX CONTROL

Event Name	Description
LinkedClicked	This event is triggered when a link is clicked.
SelectionChanged	This event is triggered when the selection changes.

TABLE 11-2 USEFUL METHODS FOR THE RICHTEXTBOX CONTROL

Name	Type	Description
DetectUrls	Read/Write	Enables URL detection. If set to True, URLs are underlined and a browser is launched when an URL is clicked.
Rtf	Read/Write	Stores the content of the RtfTextbox in RTF format.
SelectedRtf	Read/Write	The selected text in RTF format.
SelectedText	Read/Write	The selected text in plain text.
SelectionAlignment	Read/Write	The alignment of the selected text. This could be Center, Left, or Right.
SelectionColor	Read/Write	The color of the selected text.
SelectionFont	Read/Write	The font of the selected text.

Designing the Interface

The Rich Text Editor interface consists of a toolbar and a RichTextBox control, as shown in Figure 11-5. The toolbar contains the Bold, Italic, and Underline buttons. The ToolStrip control, which is implemented in a similar manner to the MenuStrip control, will be used to create a toolbar. As you follow the steps to implement the interface, you'll discover why Visual C# 2005 Express Edition is an invaluable companion to any C# programmer.

1. Create a new Windows Forms application called RichTextEditor.

2. Set the Text property of the form to Rich Text Editor.

3. Double-click on the ToolStrip control. The control is added at the top of the form.

4. Change the Name property of the ToolStrip to RichTextEditorToolstrip.

5. Click on the ToolStrip; this will select it. You'll see the drop-down box. Select the Button control from the drop-down list (see Figure 11.6). A Button control will be added to the ToolStrip. Set the Name of the Button to NewButton. Set the DisplayStyle property to Text. Set the Text property to New. The New button is added to the ToolStrip.

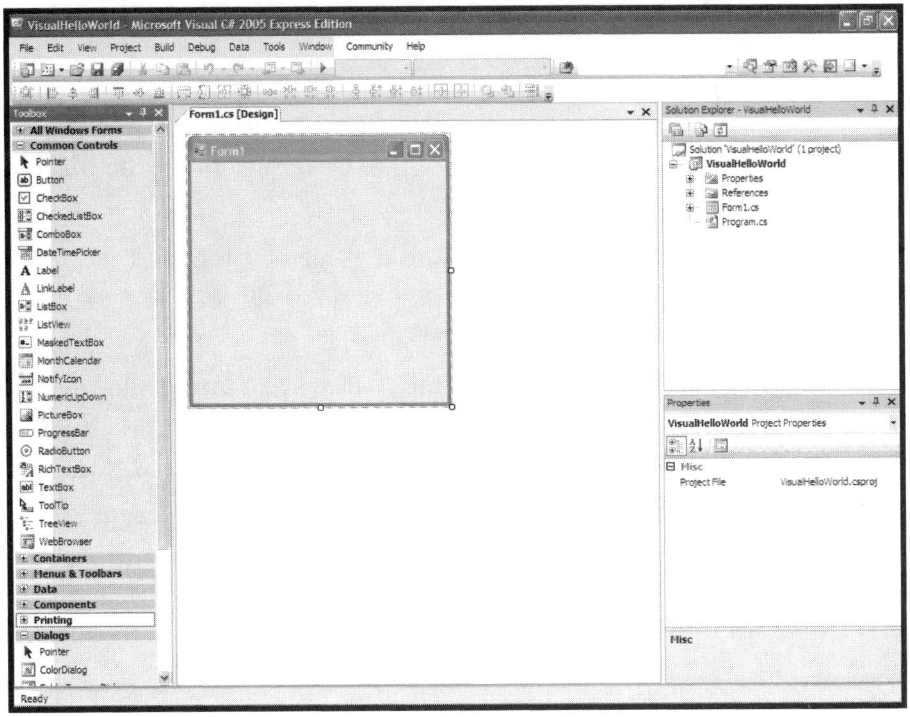

FIGURE II-5

The Rich Text Editor interface.

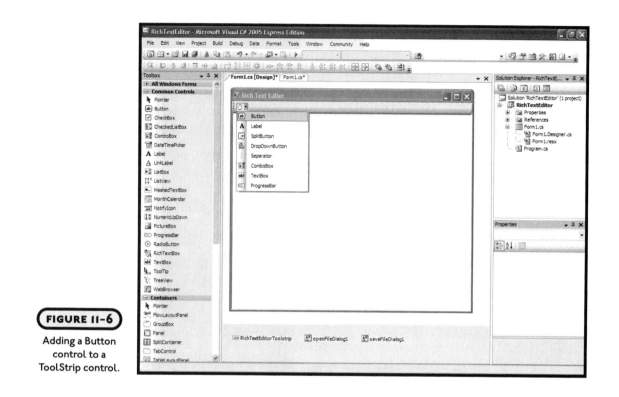

FIGURE 11-6

Adding a Button control to a ToolStrip control.

6. A drop-down box is displayed next to the New button. Add the Open button to the ToolStrip. Set the Name of the Button to OpenButton. Set the DisplayStyle property to Text. Set the Text property to Open.

7. A drop-down box is displayed next to the Open button. Add the Save As button to the ToolStrip. Set the Name of the Button to SaveAsButton. Set the DisplayStyle property to Text. Set the Text property to Save As.

8. A drop-down box is displayed next to the Save As button. Add the Bold button to the ToolStrip. Set the Name of the Button to BoldButton. Set the DisplayStyle property to Text. Set the Text property to Bold.

9. Add the Italic and Underline buttons using the same procedure.

10. Drag a RichTextBox control onto the form. Set the Name property to RichTextBoxEditor. Set the Dock property to Fill.

11. Double-click on the OpenFileDialog control. The control is added to the pane at the bottom of the Windows Form designer. The OpenFileDialog will be shown when the Open button on the toolbar is clicked.

12. Double-click on the SaveFileDialog control. The control is added to the pane at the bottom of the Windows Form designer. The SaveFileDialog will be shown when the Save As button on the toolbar is clicked.

Adding the C# Code

The interface design was simple enough, but what about writing the C# code? Well that is going to be even easier. We can call the LoadFile() and SaveFile() methods of the Rich-TextBox control to open and save RTF files. These methods preserve formatting. We need to change the SelectionFont property to get the RichTextBox control to make our formatting changes.

The following is the code to save an RTF file:

```
richTextBoxEditor.SaveFile(saveFileDialog1.FileName);
Opening an RTF file is accomplished as follows:
richTextBoxEditor.LoadFile(openFileDialog1.FileName);
```

To make selected text bold, use the following:

```
Font newFont = new
Font(richTextBoxEdit.SelectionFont,(richTextEdit.SelectionFont.Bold ?
richTextBoxEdit.SelectionFont.Style & ~FontStyle.Bold :
richTextBoxEdit.SelectionFont.Style | FontStyle.Bold));
richTextBoxEdit.SelectionFont = newFont;
```

Adding code to the application:

1. Double-click on the New button. The Form1.cs file will be displayed within the code editor. A NewButton_Click() method has also been created automatically. This method needs to clear the RichTextBox control. This is achieved by calling the Clear() method:

```
private void NewButton_Click(object sender, EventArgs e)
{
        richTextBoxEditor.Clear();
}
```

2. Click on the Form Designer tab. The Rich Text Editor interface will be displayed.

3. Double-click on the Open button. An `OpenButton_Click()` method has been created. This method needs to show the OpenFileDialog and pass the path of the RTF file to the `LoadFile()` method.

```
private void OpenButton_Click(object sender, EventArgs e)
{
        if (openFileDialog1.ShowDialog() == DialogResult.OK)
        {
                richTextBoxEditor.LoadFile(openFileDialog1.FileName);
        }
}
```

4. Click on the Form Designer tab. The Rich Text Editor interface will be displayed.

5. Double-click on the Save As button. A `SaveAsButton_Click()` method has been created. This method needs to show the SaveFileDialog and pass the path of the RTF file to the `SaveFile()` method.

```
private void SaveAsButton_Click(object sender, EventArgs e)
{
        if (saveFileDialog1.ShowDialog() == DialogResult.OK)   --bl
        {
                richTextBoxEditor.SaveFile(saveFileDialog1.FileName);    --bl
        }
}
```

6. Click on the Form Designer tab. The Rich Text Editor interface will be displayed.

7. Double-click on the Bold button. A `BoldButton_Click()` method has been created. This method needs to apply bold formatting to the selected text, if it is not already bold. If the selected text is bold, the bold formatting is disabled.

```
private void BoldButton_Click(object sender, EventArgs e)
{
        Font newFont = new
Font(richTextBoxEditor.SelectionFont,(richTextBoxEditor.SelectionFont.Bold ?
richTextBoxEditor.SelectionFont.Style & ~FontStyle.Bold :
richTextBoxEditor.SelectionFont.Style | FontStyle.Bold));
        richTextBoxEditor.SelectionFont = newFont;
}
```

8. Click on the Form Designer tab. The Rich Text Editor interface will be displayed.

9. Double-click on the Italic button. An `ItalicButton_Click()` method has been created. This method needs to apply italic formatting to the selected text, if it is not already in italics. This is very similar to making text bold.

```
private void ItalicButton_Click(object sender, EventArgs e)
{
        Font newFont = new Font(richTextBoxEditor.SelectionFont,
(richTextBoxEditor.SelectionFont.Italic ?
richTextBoxEditor.SelectionFont.Style & ~FontStyle.Italic :
richTextBoxEditor.SelectionFont.Style | FontStyle.Italic));
        richTextBoxEditor.SelectionFont = newFont;
}
```

10. Click on the Form Designer tab. The Simple Text Editor Form will be displayed.

11. Double-click on the Italic button. An `UnderlineButton_Click()` method has been created. This method needs to make the selected text underlined.

```
private void UnderlineButton_Click(object sender, EventArgs e)
{
        Font newFont = new Font(richTextBoxEditor.SelectionFont,
(richTextBoxEditor.SelectionFont.Underline ?
richTextBoxEditor.SelectionFont.Style & ~FontStyle.Underline :
richTextBoxEditor.SelectionFont.Style | FontStyle.Underline));
        richTextBoxEditor.SelectionFont = newFont;
}
```

12. That's all we need to do. We can test the application. Click on the Start button to build and compile the application. The Rich Text Editor application will be launched. We can now use it to enter and format text.

The full code listing for the Rich Text Editor:

```
using System;
using System.Collections.Generic;
using System.ComponentModel;
using System.Data;
using System.Drawing;
using System.Text;
using System.Windows.Forms;
```

```csharp
namespace RichTextEditor
{
    public partial class Form1 : Form
    {
        public Form1()
        {
            InitializeComponent();
        }

        private void NewButton_Click(object sender, EventArgs e)
        {
            RichTextBoxEditor.Clear();
        }

        private void OpenButton_Click(object sender, EventArgs e)
        {
            if (openFileDialog1.ShowDialog() == DialogResult.OK)
            {
                RichTextBoxEditor.LoadFile(openFileDialog1.FileName);
            }
        }

        private void SaveAsButton_Click(object sender, EventArgs e)
        {
            if (saveFileDialog1.ShowDialog() == DialogResult.OK)
            {
                RichTextBoxEditor.SaveFile(saveFileDialog1.FileName);
            }
        }

        private void BoldButton_Click(object sender, EventArgs e)
        {
            Font newFont = new Font(RichTextBoxEditor.SelectionFont,
(RichTextBoxEditor.SelectionFont.Bold ? RichTextBoxEditor.SelectionFont.Style &
~FontStyle.Bold : RichTextBoxEditor.SelectionFont.Style | FontStyle.Bold));
            RichTextBoxEditor.SelectionFont = newFont;
        }
```

```csharp
        private void ItalicButton_Click(object sender, EventArgs e)
        {
                Font newFont = new Font(RichTextBoxEditor.SelectionFont,
(RichTextBoxEditor.SelectionFont.Italic ? RichTextBoxEditor.SelectionFont.Style &
~FontStyle.Italic : RichTextBoxEditor.SelectionFont.Style | FontStyle.Italic));
                RichTextBoxEditor.SelectionFont = newFont;
        }

        private void UnderlineButton_Click(object sender, EventArgs e)
        {
                Font newFont = new Font(RichTextBoxEditor.SelectionFont,
(RichTextBoxEditor.SelectionFont.Underline ? RichTextBoxEditor.SelectionFont.Style &
~FontStyle.Underline : RichTextBoxEditor.SelectionFont.Style | FontStyle.Underline));
                RichTextBoxEditor.SelectionFont = newFont;
        }
    }
}
```

Testing the Application

We are going to take a structured approach to testing and use a test plan that is shown next. A test plan is a list of everything that we need to test. It could be a step-by-step guide to performing a test or simply a checklist for everything that needs to be tested.

Test Plan for the Rich Text Editor

- Create and save a new RTF file.
- Open an existing RTF file.
- Create a new file. Enter three paragraphs. Format each paragraph with a different format. The first paragraph could be bold, the second could be italic, and the third could be underlined.
- Format a text selection with all three formatting options; in other words, make the selected text bold, italic, and underlined.
- Open a saved RTF file in Microsoft Word. Change the color, font, and font size of the text. Save the file as an RTF file. Open the file in the Rich Text Editor. The Rich-TextBox control is capable of displaying RTF files edited in Microsoft Word.

Summary

This chapter has provided a comprehensive introduction to the functionality contained within the System.IO namespace. You used the System.IO.File class to create, copy, move, and delete files. You also used the System.IO.Directory class to create, move, and delete folders. You built a Simple Text Editor application that uses the Open and Save As dialog boxes. Finally, you built a Rich Text Editor application that is able to save and open RTF files.

Challenges

1. Design a Windows Forms application that allows you to copy and delete files and folders.

2. Write a program that recursively lists the content of a folder.

3. Use a Tree control to display the contents of a folder recursively.

4. Write a program that calculates in megabytes (MB) the amount of free space that is available on your hard drive (C drive).

5. Enhance the Rich Text Editor application so that a user can change the font, font size, and the color of text.

C# AND ASP.NET WEB SITES

here are thousands of portals, Web sites, and personal Web logs dedicated to the .NET Framework, C#, and ASP.NET. This appendix presents some good starting places. Use these resources to extend your C# and programming knowledge. Become part of a community. When you are having trouble, ask questions. When you have a solution, share it with others. Your journey as a C# programmer has just begun!

C# WEB SITES

The following Web sites focus on C#:

Microsoft Visual C# Developer Center	http://msdn.microsoft.com/vcsharp/team/default.aspx
C# Help	http://www.csharphelp.com
C# Station	http://www.csharp-station.com/
C# Corner	http://www.csharp-corner.com/
The Code Project	http://www.codeproject.com/
GotDotNet	http://www.gotdotnet.com/
cshrp.net	http://www.cshrp.net/
.NET 247	http://www.dotnet247.com/247reference/default.aspx

| CSharpFriends | http://www.csharpfriends.com/ |
| CodeGuru | http://www.codeguru.com/ |

OPEN SOURCE C# SOFTWARE

The following are some useful C# open source applications:

C# Open Source Applications	http://csharp-source.net/
csUnit—unit testing tool for the Microsoft .NET Framework	http://www.csunit.org/index.php
SharpDevelop—C# IDE	http://www.icsharpcode.net/opensource/sd/
Perspective—wiki engine	http://www.high-beyond.com
.Text—blogging engine	http://www.gotdotnet.com/Community/Workspaces/Workspace.aspx?id=e99fccb3-1a8c-42b5-90ee-348f6b77c407

ASP.NET WEB SITES

The following are popular sites that include tutorials on using C# to build ASP.NET Web applications:

Microsoft ASP.NET	http://www.asp.net/
123aspx	http://www.123aspx.com/
DevASP.Net	http://www.devasp.net/
4GuysFromRolla	http://www.4guysfromrolla.com/
ASPNet101	http://www.aspnet101.com/aspnet101/default.aspx
angryCoder	http://www.angrycoder.com/
ASP101	http://www.asp101.com/aspdotnet/default.asp
15 Seconds	http://www.15seconds.com/
ASPAlliance	http://aspalliance.com/

Index

Symbols

+ (addition operator), 24, 96
&& (And operator), 46
{ } (curly braces), 22
( ) (parentheses), 25
/ (division operator), 24
// (double slashes), 29
= (equal sign), 9, 27
> (greater than operator), 45
>= (greater than or equal to operator), 45
== (is equal to operator), 45, 97
< (less than operator), 45
<= (less than or equal to operator), 45
% (modulus operator), 24
* (multiplication operator), 24
!= (not equal to operator), 45, 97
! (Not operator), 46–47
|| (Or operator), 46–47
( ) (parentheses), 25
. (period), 9
" (quotation marks), 28
; (semicolon), 9, 12, 21–22, 26
- (subtraction operator), 24

A

Abs() method, 99
ACos() method, 99
addition operator (+), 24, 96
Align command (Format menu), 72
alignment, form controls, 72
All Programs command (Start menu), 4
And operator (&&), 46

animation and collision detection, 131–133
appending data to files, 227
arithmetic. *See* math operations
arrays
    data types of, 101
    explained, 100
    initialization, 101–102
    length, 101
    multidimensional, 103–104
    sorting, 102–103
    two-dimensional, 103
ascending sort order, arrays, 102
ASin() method, 99
ATan() method, 99
ATan2() method, 99

B

BackColor property, Windows Forms application, 68
background colors, form design, 68
BackgroundImage property, Windows Forms application, 68
binding data to form controls, 186–187
blank form, Windows Forms application, 5
BMP image format, 2
bold font style, 124
bool keyword, 29
boolean variables, 29
borders, form design, 82
break keyword, 56
breakpoints, 202